Characterization of Mercury Contamination in the Androscoggin River, Coos County, New Hampshire

By Ann T. Chalmers, Mark C. Marvin-DiPasquale, James R. Degnan, James F. Coles, Jennifer L. Agee, and Darryl Luce

Prepared in cooperation with the U.S. Environmental Protection Agency

Open-File Report 2013–1076

U.S. Department of the Interior
U.S. Geological Survey

U.S. Department of the Interior
SALLY JEWELL, Secretary

U.S. Geological Survey
Suzette M. Kimball, Acting Director

U.S. Geological Survey, Reston, Virginia: 2013

For more information on the USGS—the Federal source for science about the Earth, its natural and living resources, natural hazards, and the environment, visit http://www.usgs.gov or call 1–888–ASK–USGS.

For an overview of USGS information products, including maps, imagery, and publications, visit http://www.usgs.gov/pubprod

To order this and other USGS information products, visit http://store.usgs.gov

Suggested citation:
Chalmers, A.T., Marvin-DiPasquale, M.C., Degnan, J.R., Coles, J.F., Agee, J.L., and Luce, Darryl, 2013, Characterization of mercury contamination in the Androscoggin River, Coos County, New Hampshire: U.S. Geological Survey Open-File Report 2013–1076, 56 p., http://pubs.usgs.gov/of/2013/1076/.

Acknowledgments

The authors would like to thank the many individuals that provided field and laboratory support for this project. Andrew Hoffman of the New Hampshire Department of Environmental Services (NHDES), Vivien Taylor of Dartmouth College, and Cornell Rosiu of the U.S. Environmental Protection Agency (USEPA) assisted with sediment collection; Chuck Dobroski of Avatar Environmental, Kenneth Munney of the U.S. Fish and Wildlife Service, and Stan Pauwels of the USEPA collected fish samples; David Buck of BioDiversity Research Institute collected bat samples; and Michael Ferrier, Erica Czerepak, and Bethany Kelley of USEPA Region 1 Environmental Services Assistance Team (ESAT) collected oligochaete, swallow, and toxicity samples and processed the surface and pore-water toxicity samples.

Thor Smith of the U.S. Geological Survey (USGS) assisted with surface-water, pore-water, and invertebrate sampling. Marc Zimmerman, Jon Denner, and Jamie Shanley of the USGS assisted with pore-water sample collection, and Evangelos Kakouros, Le Kieu, and Michelle Beyer of the USGS analyzed pore-water and sediment samples. Jeffrey Deacon of the USGS and Cornell Rosiu of the USEPA were instrumental in the study planning and design. The authors would also like to thank Chuck Dobroski and Jamie Shanley for their thoughtful technical reviews.

Contents

Figures

Tables

Conversion Factors and Datum

SI to Inch/Pound

Multiply	By	To obtain
Length		
centimeter (cm)	0.3937	inch (in.)
meter (m)	3.281	foot (ft)
kilometer (km)	0.6214	mile (mi)
meter (m)	1.094	yard (yd)
Area		
square meter (m^2)	0.0002471	acre
square meter (m^2)	10.76	square foot (ft^2)
square centimeter (cm^2)	0.1550	square inch (ft^2)
square kilometer (km^2)	0.3861	square mile (mi^2)
Mass		
kilogram (kg)	2.205	pound avoirdupois (lb)
Hydraulic gradient		
meter per kilometer (m/km)	5.27983	foot per mile (ft/mi)

In this report, the words right and left refer to directions that would be reported by an observer facing downstream.

Vertical coordinate information is referenced to the North American Vertical Datum of 1988 (NAVD 88).

Horizontal coordinate information is referenced to the North American Datum of 1983 (NAD 83).

Altitude, as used in this report, refers to distance above the vertical datum.

Concentrations of chemical constituents in water are either in milligrams per liter (mg/L), micrograms per liter (µg/L), nanograms per liter (ng/L), moles per liter (M), or millimoles per liter (mmol/L).

Characterization of Mercury Contamination in the Androscoggin River, Coos County, New Hampshire

By Ann T. Chalmers[1], Mark C. Marvin-DiPasquale[1], James R. Degnan[1], James F. Coles[1], Jennifer L. Agee[1], and Darryl Luce[2]

Abstract

The former chloralkali facility in Berlin, New Hampshire, was designated a Superfund site in 2005. Historic paper mill activities resulted in the contamination of groundwater, surface water, and sediments with many organic compounds and mercury (Hg). Hg continues to seep into the Androscoggin River in elemental form through bedrock fractures. The objective of this study was to spatially characterize (1) the extent of Hg contamination in water, sediment, and biota; (2) Hg speciation and methylmercury (MeHg) production potential rates in sediment; (3) the availability of inorganic divalent Hg (Hg(II)) for Hg(II)-methylation (MeHg production); and (4) ancillary sediment geochemistry necessary to better understand Hg speciation and MeHg production potential rates in this system.

Concentrations of total mercury (THg) and MeHg in sediment, pore water, and biota in the Androscoggin River were elevated downstream from the former chloralkali facility compared with those upstream from reference sites. Sequential extraction of surface sediment showed a distinct difference in Hg speciation upstream compared with downstream from the contamination site. An upstream site was dominated by potassium hydroxide-extractable forms (for example, organic-Hg or particle-bound Hg(II)), whereas sites downstream from the point source were dominated by more chemically recalcitrant forms (largely concentrated nitric acid-extractable), indicative of elemental mercury or mercurous chloride. At all sites, only a minor fraction (less than 0.1 percent) of THg existed in chemically labile forms (for example, water extractable or weak acid extractable). All metrics indicated that a greater percentage of mercury at an upstream site was available for Hg(II)-methylation compared with sites downstream from the point source, but the absolute concentration of bioavailable Hg(II) was greater downstream from the point source. In addition, the concentration of tin-reducible inorganic reactive mercury, a surrogate measure of bioavailable Hg(II) generally increased with distance downstream from the point source. Whereas concentrations of mercury species on a sediment-dry-weight basis generally reflected the relative location of the sample to the point source, river-reach integrated mercury-species inventories and MeHg production potential (MPP) rates reflected the amount of fine-grained sediment in a given reach.

THg concentrations in biota were significantly higher downstream from the point source compared with upstream reference sites for smallmouth bass, white sucker, crayfish, oligochaetes, bat fur, nestling tree swallow blood and feathers, adult tree swallow blood, and tree swallow eggs. As with tin-reducible inorganic reactive mercury, THg in smallmouth bass also increased with distance downstream from the point source. Toxicity tests and invertebrate community assessments suggested that invertebrates were not impaired at the current (2009 and 2010) levels of mercury contamination downstream from the point source. Concentrations of THg and MeHg in most water and sediment samples from the Androscoggin River were below U.S. Environmental Protection Agency (USEPA), the Canadian Council of Ministers of the Environment, and probable effects level guidelines. Surface-water and sediment samples from the Androscoggin River had similar THg concentrations but lower MeHg concentrations compared with other rivers in the region. Concentrations of THg in fish tissue were all above regional and U.S. Environmental Protection Agency guidelines. Moreover, median THg concentrations in smallmouth bass from the Androscoggin River were significantly higher than those reported in regional surveys of river and streams nationwide and in the Northeastern United States and Canada. The higher concentrations of mercury in smallmouth bass suggest conditions may be more favorable for Hg(II)-methylation and bioaccumulation in the Androscoggin River compared with many other rivers in the United States and Canada.

[1]U.S. Geological Survey.

[2]U.S. Environmental Protection Agency.

Introduction

During operation of the chloralkali facility in Berlin, New Hampshire, elemental mercury (Hg^0) was spilled contaminating the overburden and underlying fractured rock on the east (left) bank of the Androscoggin River. Hg^0 is relatively nontoxic; the primary pathway of Hg^0 toxicity in the environment begins with the oxidation to inorganic divalent mercury (Hg(II)) in the presence of chloride, thiol compounds, and oxygen. In low salinity waters such as those of the Androscoggin River, Hg^0 oxidation is quite slow, and formation of oxidation products on the surface of the liquid further reduces oxidation rates (Amyot and others, 2005). The conversion of Hg(II) to more bioavailable methylmercury (MeHg) is a process that is largely carried out by anaerobic bacteria near the sediment-water interface (Gilmour and others, 1992). Rates of net benthic MeHg production in the sediments are controlled by the activity of the Hg(II)-methylating microbial community and by Hg(II) availability to microbes (Marvin-DiPasquale and others, 2009a). Environmental factors that affect the activity of communities of Hg(II)-methylating bacteria include temperature, pH, and presence of suitable electron acceptors and donors. Availability of Hg(II) to microbes is controlled by total mercury (THg) concentration, dissolved organic carbon (DOC), sediment grain size, and calcium, iron, and sulfur solid-phase mineral chemistry. Understanding the Hg(II) processes and the environments that are conducive to methylation will provide key information for remedial actions and decisions.

Site History and Previous Work

In September 2005, Congress added the former chloralkali facility in Berlin, N.H., to the national priorities list, commonly known as the Superfund list (U.S. Environmental Protection Agency, 2005). Investigations onsite have revealed elevated mercury, lead, arsenic, polycyclic aromatic hydrocarbons, organochlorine chemicals (dioxin and furans, polychlorinated biphenyls), and other toxic metals in groundwater and soils (Darryl Luce, U.S. Environmental Protection Agency (USEPA), written commun., 2008). The mercury contamination originates from two longstanding point sources across from one another on the Androscoggin River in Berlin, N.H. A chloralkali facility that produced chlorine gas for the papermaking industry using electrolytic diaphragm cells operated from the late 1800s through the 1960s (Margaret Bastien, New Hampshire Department of Environmental Services (NHDES), written commun., 2004). How mercury was used at the facility is uncertain. Mercury may have been used in the cells to separate chlorine from a brine solution. The second source of mercury was from a sawmill that used mercuric chloride wood preserving process known as kyanization. Kyanization was used by the sawmill from 1888 through 1930 (Weston Solutions, 2005). The mercuric chloride may have been prepared at the chloralkali facility and then transported across

the river for use at the kyanization plant. Regardless of use, the main release of mercury to the environment was at the chloralkali facility on the left bank of the Androscoggin River, just downstream from Sawmill Dam (fig. 1). The total amount of mercury released from the facility that seeped into the overburden and into the underlying fractured bedrock is unknown (Degnan and others, 2005). Efforts to contain the mercury at the chloralkali site and eliminate seepage to the river include demolition of the cell houses, installation of a bentonite-soil slurry barrier wall on the site perimeter, and pressure grouting the bedrock along the riverbank (Margaret Bastien, NHDES, written commun., 2003). Despite earlier actions to address the source of contamination, mercury continues to seep into the Androscoggin River through fractures in the bedrock at the edge of the site (Darryl Luce, USEPA, written commun., 2008). Mercury has also been found in the sediment of the adjacent Androscoggin River from sampling conducted by the former site owners and the NHDES (Darryl Luce, USEPA, written commun., 2008). THg concentrations (average plus or minus standard deviation) in sediments collected at dam impoundments by the NHDES (Lori Siegel, NHDES, written commun., 2004) were highly variable, from 75 ±177 nanograms per gram (ng/g) at Sawmill Dam (upstream from the facility) to 361 ±483 ng/g at Riverside Dam and 354 ±277 ng/g at Smith Hydro Dam (both downstream from the facility). MeHg concentrations in sediments collected by the NHDES were lowest at Sawmill Dam (0.071 ±0.082 ng/g) and higher at Smith Hydro Dam (1.00 ±0.79 ng/g) and Riverside Dam (1.28 ±2.16 ng/g). Subsequently, further investigation into the extent of mercury contamination and transformation processes within the Androscoggin River was deemed warranted by the USEPA to determine the potential impacts on the environment and to provide a more comprehensive understanding of mercury dynamics in this system to guide potential remediation activities. To that end, the USEPA funded a study conducted by the U.S. Geological Survey (USGS) from 2009 through 2012 to provide more detailed information regarding the extent of mercury contamination and speciation within the Androscoggin River. The major objectives of this study were to characterize the extent of mercury contamination in sediment, water, and biota of the Androscoggin River and to assess mercury speciation and the potential availability of in-situ mercury for Hg(II)-methylation.

Purpose and Scope

This report (1) compares surface-water, pore-water, sediment, and biota THg and MeHg concentrations upstream and downstream from a former chloralkali facility; (2) evaluates the potential for Hg(II)-methylation and mercury bioaccumulation; (3) explains differences in MeHg production rates and bioavailable Hg(II) patterns among sites using nonparametric rank sum tests and best-fit linear model equations; (4) assesses the health of the aquatic ecosystem surrounding the former chloralkali facility using a variety of surface-water, sediment,

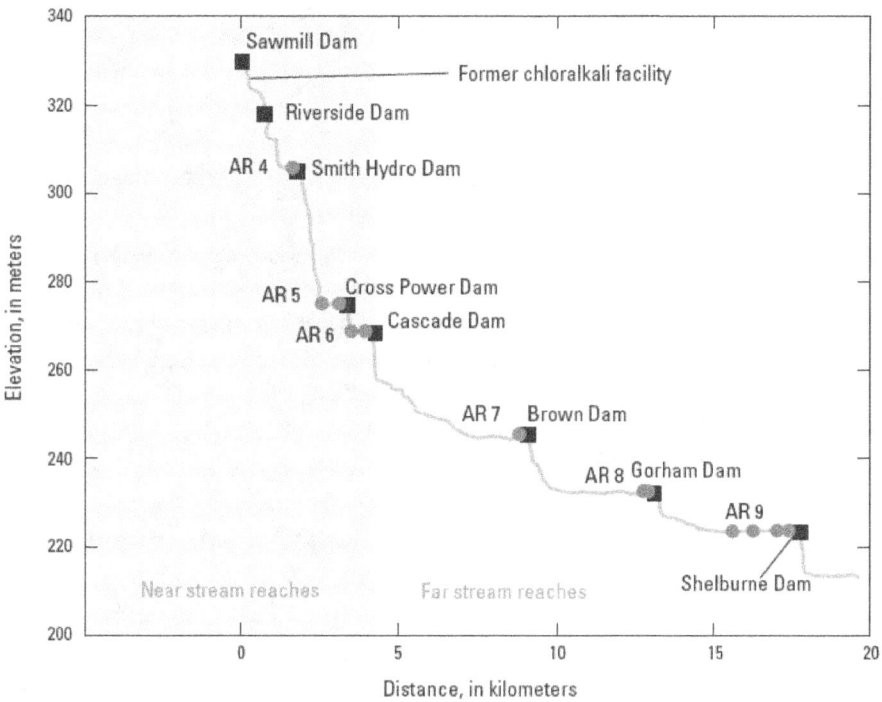

Figure 1. Generalized locations of sediment and pore-water sampling sites on the Androscoggin River downstream from a former chloralkali facility in Berlin, New Hampshire. Stream reaches are signified by AR followed by number. The reference reach (AR2) is 16 kilometers upstream from the former chloralkali facility and is not shown. Sampling locations are indicated by red circles, dams are indicated by black squares. Elevation and distance data from Google Earth, February 17, 2012.

and biological indices and guidelines; and (5) compares THg and MeHg concentrations in water, sediment, and biota from the study site to concentrations reported in other river systems nationally and regionally in the Northeastern United States and Canada.

In addition, this report also summarizes concurrent bio-monitoring data collected by BioDiversity Research Institute (Gorham, Maine) and Avatar Environmental (West Chester, Pennsylvania) contracted by the USEPA for the purposes of providing additional context regarding the human health and ecological impacts of mercury within the study area.

Study Approach and Methods

The study area encompasses a 40-kilometer (km) reach of the Androscoggin River from Pontook Reservoir to just upstream from Shelburne Dam, including the former chlor-alkali facility site in Berlin (table 1, fig. 2). Individual river reaches (coded as AR followed by the number of the reach#) were defined by the presence of dam structures at the upper and lower boundary of each reach. The precise coordinates for all sampling locations are listed in table 2–1. Pontook

Reservoir (AR1) and Wheeler Bay (within the upper portion of AR2), both upstream from the facility, were used as reference sites of background (nonpoint-source) conditions. AR1 was used as a reference site for birds and bats, whereas AR2 was a reference site for sediment, pore water, surface water, epifaunal invertebrates, crayfish, and birds. Seven stream reaches, from the facility (within AR3) to just upstream from Shelburne Dam (AR9), were sampled to characterize the mercury contamination downstream from the point source.

THg and MeHg concentrations were analyzed in surface water, pore water, and sediment and THg in macroinvertebrates, crayfish, fish, bats, and birds (tables 1, A2–1). The potential for Hg(II)-methylation and MeHg bioaccumulation was assessed by a number of different metrics. The percentage of THg as MeHg (percent MeHg) in sediment was used as a proxy for Hg(II)-methylation efficiency. Tin-reducible reactive inorganic mercury ($Hg(II)_R$) was used as a surrogate for the pool of inorganic Hg(II) readily available to sediment bacteria for Hg(II)-methylation. This methodologically defined assay measures simple Hg(II)-salts, such as mercury sulfate and mercury chloride Hg(II) bound to low molecular weight organic ligands, and Hg(II) weakly adsorbed to particle surfaces (Marvin-DiPasquale and others, 2006; Marvin-DiPasquale,

Table 1.   Study sampling area description and dates for the Androscoggin River from Pontook Reservoir to Shelburne Dam, New Hampshire.

[Epifaunal invertebrates were collected in rock baskets]

Reach code	Reach description	Sampling dates	Sample types
AR1	Above Pontook Dam	2010	Bat, bird
AR2	Pontook Dam to Wheeler Bay	2009, 2010, 2011	Sediment, pore-water, surface-water, epifaunal invertebrate, oligochaetes, crayfish, fish, bird
AR3	Sawmill Dam to Riverside Dam	2009, 2010	Surface-water, epifaunal invertebrate, crayfish, fish, bird
AR4	Riverside Dam to Smith Hydro Dam	2009, 2010	Sediment, pore-water, surface-water, epifaunal invertebrate, oligochaetes, crayfish, fish, bird
AR5	Smith Hydro Dam to Cross Power Dam	2010, 2011	Sediment, pore-water, oligochaetes, crayfish, fish
AR6	Cross Power Dam to Cascade Dam	2009, 2010, 2011	Sediment, pore-water, oligochaetes, crayfish, fish
AR7	Cascade Dam to Brown Dam	2010, 2011	Sediment, pore-water, oligochaetes, crayfish, fish
AR8	Brown Dam to Gorham Dam	2009, 2010	Sediment, pore-water, surface-water, epifaunal invertebrate, oligochaetes, crayfish, fish, bird
AR9	Gorham Dam to Shelburne Dam	2009, 2010	Sediment, pore-water, surface-water, epifaunal invertebrate, oligochaetes, crayfish, fish, bat, bird

unpub. data). Microbial MeHg production potential (MPP) rates were measured in sediment using ^{200}Hg(II) stable isotope incubations to measure the microbial rate constant for Hg(II)-methylation (k_{meth}) and calculated based on k_{meth} and the independently measured Hg(II)$_R$ concentration (Marvin-DiPasquale and others, 2008). Another approach used to assess mercury availability was a five-step sequential extraction (Bloom and others, 2003) that chemically characterizes the THg pool from most labile (water-extractable) to most refractory (aqua regia-extractable). Site-specific differences in MPP rates were examined in terms of a suite of environmental factors, such as sediment redox conditions, particle size, sulfur and iron chemistry, and organic content in sediment, all of which can affect both the activity of Hg(II)-methylating bacteria and the availability of Hg(II) to those bacteria.

The potential biological impact of the mercury contamination in the study area was assessed by the community composition of epifaunal macroinvertebrate assemblages and toxicity testing of surface waters, pore waters, and bulk sediment. Surface-water, sediment, and biological indices and guidelines were also used to evaluate the potential ecological impact of the mercury contamination within the study area.

Field Methods

Field sampling was performed during 3 years (table 1). Samples were collected from a wide range of media during August and September 2009, including surface water, sediment pore water, whole sediment, fish, crayfish, epifaunal invertebrates, and infaunal invertebrates. Surface-water, sediment pore-water, and whole-sediment samples were

collected by the USGS, fish and crayfish were collected by Avatar Environmental, and epifaunal invertebrates and infaunal invertebrates were collected by USGS and USEPA Region 1 Environmental Services Assistance Team (ESAT). During August 2010, USGS field sampling focused on mercury speciation and Hg(II)-methylation in sediment and on ancillary sediment parameters associated with carbon, iron, and sulfur. Additional biological sampling was conducted during 2010 and 2011 by BioDiversity Research Institute, ESAT, and the USEPA and included fish, infaunal invertebrates, bats, and marsh birds.

Surface-Water Sampling

Surface-water samples were collected during low streamflow conditions (average daily flow of 1,620 cubic feet per second) in September 2009 using multiple sampling points, based on standard USGS protocols (U.S. Geological Survey, 2005), and were processed using trace-metal clean techniques (Olson and DeWild, 1999). At wadeable sections of the river, samples were collected with a hand-held teflon depth integrating sampler (DH–81). At nonwadeable sections, samples were collected using an isokinetic sampler (D–95; equipped with a teflon nozzle and a teflon bottle) that was lowered from bridges using a reel and cable. Specific conductance, pH, dissolved oxygen, and water temperature were determined during the collection of surface-water samples using a multiprobe sonde (YSI 600XL). Samples were filtered using 0.45-micrometer (µm) high-capacity capsule filters. Both dissolved (filter passing) and total (nonfiltered) surface-water samples were collected during 2009; THg and MeHg

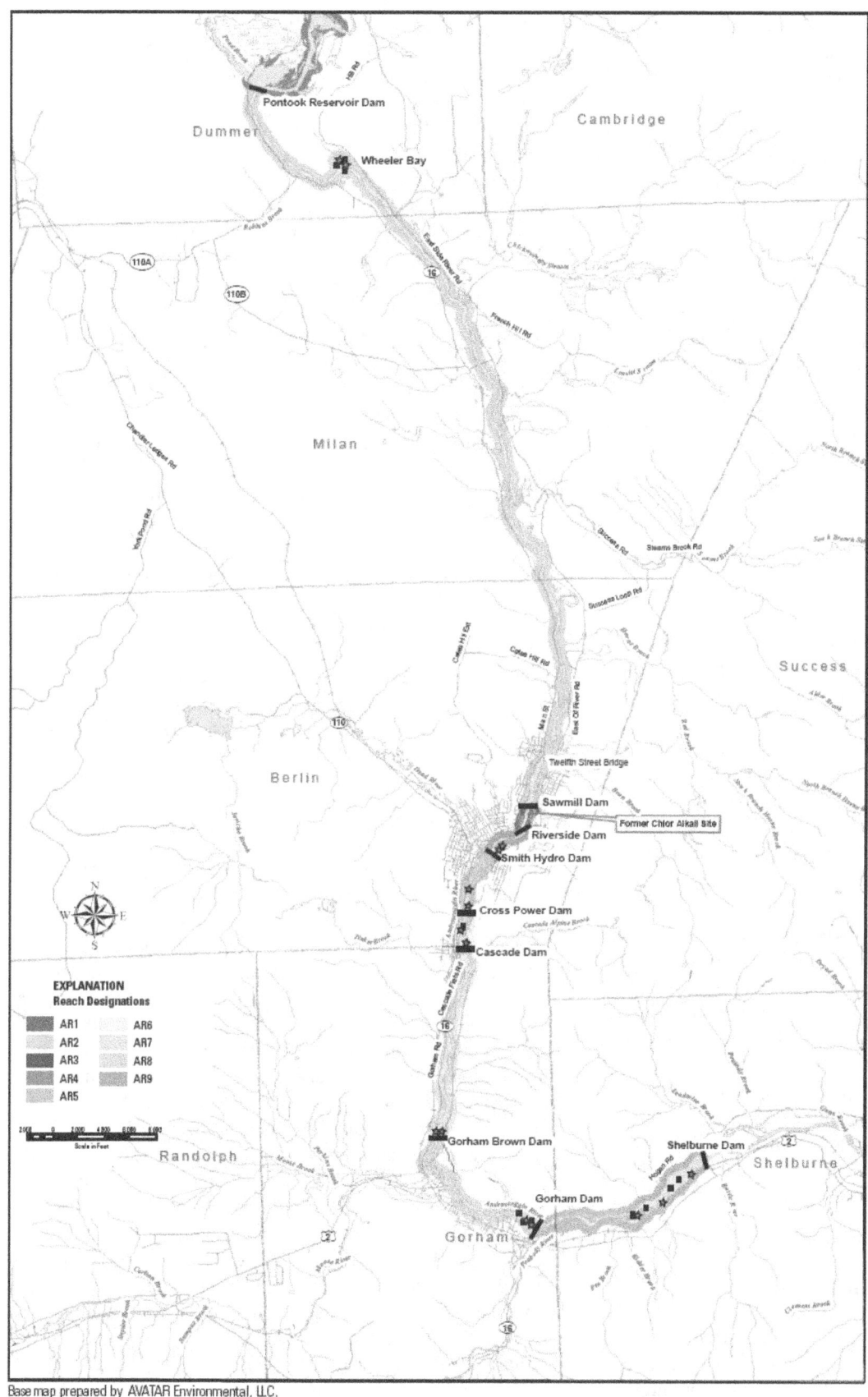

Figure 2.   Map of study area on the Androscoggin River, Coos County, New Hampshire. Stream reaches are signified by AR followed by number. Pore-water and sediment sampling sites are black squares (2009) and red stars (2010). Base map prepared by AVATAR Environmental LCC.

samples were preserved with hydrochloric acid to a pH of less than 2, total recoverable metals (antimony, arsenic, beryllium, cadmium, chromium, copper, lead, nickel, selenium, strontium, vanadium, and zinc) samples were preserved with nitric acid to a pH of less than 2, and organic carbon samples were preserved with sulfuric acid to a pH of less than 2. All samples were kept chilled in coolers with wet ice and then refrigerated upon return to the laboratory.

Sediment Pore-Water Sampling

Pore-water samples were collected in depositional areas of the stream channel, typically along the channel margins. Pore-water samples were obtained in-situ during low stream-flow conditions during September 2009 and August 2010 using a push-point sampler as described in Zimmerman and others (2005) and were processed using trace-metal clean techniques (Olson and DeWild, 1999). A push-point sampler is designed to sample pore water with minimal disturbance to the sediment matrix. Specific conductance was used to monitor chemical differences between surface water and pore water during sampling and to verify that surface water was not drawn down into the pore-water sampling zone.

Other field parameters measured with the YSI 600XL multiprobe sonde included pH, dissolved oxygen, oxidation-reduction (redox) potential (ORP), and water temperature. ORP was measured with a platinum band electrode. Pore-water samples were collected at depths between 7 and 15 centimeters (cm) below the interface between the sediment and surface water using a peristaltic pump with teflon tubing. In-line filtration with 0.45-μm high-capacity capsule filters was used during 2009, and 0.4-μm precombusted quartz-fiber filters in teflon filter assemblies were used during 2010. Both dissolved (filter passing) and nonfiltered pore-water samples collected during 2009 were preserved for THg and MeHg (pw.THg and pw.MeHg), total recoverable metals (antimony, arsenic, beryllium, cadmium, chromium, copper, lead, nickel, selenium, strontium, vanadium, and zinc), and dissolved organic carbon (pw.DOC), as described above for surface water. All samples collected during 2010 were filtered and preserved immediately upon collection as follows: pw.THg and pw.MeHg with 6 moles per liter (M) hydrochloric acid (1 percent final concentration), ferrous iron (pw.Fe(II)) with 10 percent hydrochloric acid (2 percent final concentration), pw.DOC with phosphoric acid to a pH less than 2, and pore-water sulfate (pw.SO$_4$) was frozen.

Streambed-Sediment Sampling

Streambed-sediment samples were collected from undisturbed, continuously wetted, depositional zones in the stream channel that coincided with pore-water sampling locations (table 2–1). Samples collected during 2009 were composites of 5 to 10 representative subsamples over a 5- to 10-square meter (m^2) area of relatively homogeneous sediment

(Shelton and Capel, 1994). The upper 0- to 10-cm-depth interval of streambed sediment was sampled with a hand-held glass coring device, except at water depth greater than 1 meter (m) where an Eckman dredge was used. Samples collected for THg and MeHg were frozen onsite, whereas all other sediment samples were kept chilled on wet ice.

Streambed-sediment samples were collected during 2010 from one or two sediment cores (0- to 10-cm depth) per site as described in Lutz and others (2008). To better document spatial variability, both on a small scale around each site as well as on a larger scale between stream reaches, two to three primary sites per reach were sampled (for a total of 15 primary sites), plus three additional field replicate sediment samples collected within 10 to 50 m from each primary site (for a total of 45 field replicate sites; table 2–1). For each sampling location (primary and field replicate; total of 60 sampling sites), sediment was composited in a ziplock bag and kept cold and dark on wet ice in a cooler until further processed and subsampled (within 8 hours of sample collection). Sediment sample processing included homogenizing, subsampling, and preserving as appropriate for each analyte. Sediment ORP and pH were measured by standard electrochemical probe techniques (Marvin-DiPasquale and Agee, 2003). Incubations associated with benthic MPP rates were initiated within 8 hours of sample collection, as described below. Subsamples collected for organic content (as percent loss on ignition (percent LOI)), grain size less than 63 μm (percent fines), porosity, dry weight, and bulk density were stored chilled on wet ice. All other subsamples were frozen.

Toxicity Tests

Surface-water and pore-water toxicity tests were conducted by the USEPA Region 1 ESAT of North Chelmsford, Massachusetts. Surface water (10–12 liters (L)) was collected for chronic, 7-day bioassays with larval fathead minnow (*Pimephales promelas*) and the cladoceran (*Ceriodaphnia dubia*) using survival, growth, and reproductive criteria (U.S. Environmental Protection Agency, 2008a, b). At least 1 L of pore water was collected at each site, which was used for acute, 96-hour survival bioassays conducted using the freshwater amphipod (*Hyalella Azteca*) and the larval midge (*Chironomus tentans*), as described by the U.S. Environmental Protection Agency (2001a). Detailed methods of pore-water and surface-water toxicity testing are described by Environmental Services Assistance Team (2009a, 2009b, respectively). Whole-sediment toxicity tests were run by EnviroSystems, Inc., of Hampton, N.H. Sediment samples were collected at locations coincident with pore-water samples and were used for bulk sediment toxicity tests with the *Hyalella azteca* (28-day exposure) and *Chironomus dilutus* (20-day exposure) using survival- and growth-based criteria as described by EnviroSystems, Inc., (2010a, 2010b, respectively). All surface-water, pore-water, and bulk-sediment samples collected for toxicity tests were kept chilled on wet ice or refrigerated until use in the above bioassays.

Epifaunal Invertebrate Assemblages

Epifaunal invertebrate samples were collected following NHDES benthic index of biotic integrity (B–IBI) protocols (New Hampshire Department of Environmental Services, 2004). Rock baskets (16.5 cm × 28 cm) containing 3.8- to 7.6-cm-diameter gravel were placed in riffle habitats upstream from water-chemistry sampling sites at water depths deep enough to maintain continuous flow over the artificial substrate. Four baskets per site were anchored to the streambed by sections of steel reinforcing rod (rebar) that were approximately 1.2 m long and 19 millimeters (mm) in diameter. Invertebrate samples collected from three of the four rock baskets were used to evaluate the aquatic ecosystem health, which is based on the presence of certain taxa and the abundance of organisms at the sampling sites. The organisms collected from the fourth rock basket at each site were combined in a single sample that was analyzed for THg. The rock baskets were deployed August 6–7, 2009, and retrieved 6.5 weeks later (September 21–22, 2009).

Rock baskets were retrieved by placing a 500-mesh D-frame net downstream from the rock basket and gently lifting and sliding the rock basket into the net. Rock baskets were emptied into 500-μm sieve buckets. The empty basket cages were gently scrubbed and rinsed into 5-gallon pails, and the contents were poured into the sieve bucket. Rocks in the sieve buckets were gently brushed and rinsed to remove organisms and detritus and returned to basket cage. Leaves and detritus in the sieve bucket were rinsed, inspected for organisms, and returned to the stream. The contents of the sieve bucket were transferred to jars and preserved with 70-percent ethanol. Samples for tissue chemistry were thoroughly rinsed with site water, placed in glass jars, and frozen for subsequent analysis of THg using a Milestone direct mercury analyzer (DMA) at the USEPA laboratory in Chelmsford, Mass. Invertebrate assemblage samples were processed according to NHDES B–IBI protocols (New Hampshire Department of Environmental Services, 2004) with a 300-organism count and identified to genus and species level by Lotic, Inc., of Unity, Maine.

Infaunal Invertebrate Tissue

Infaunal worms (*Oligochaeta spp.*) were collected from the top 15 cm of sediment in the same locations as the pore-water and sediment samples. A minimum of 5 grams (g) of infaunal worms were washed of external sediment and debris, placed in glass jars, and frozen. Tissue samples were analyzed for THg using a DMA at the U.S. Department of Energy National Renewable Energy Laboratory in North Chelmsford (Nobis Engineering, 2009).

White Sucker, Smallmouth Bass, and Crayfish

Fish samples were collected by Avatar Environmental using electroshocking during August 2009 and by the U.S. Fish and Wildlife Service, the USEPA, and ESAT using rod and reel and gill nets during August 2011 (Nobis Engineering, 2009). Two whole-body composite samples of white sucker (*Catostomus commersoni*) were collected at three stream reaches during 2009 (table 1). Composite white sucker samples consisted of two to five fish. During 2011, individual whole-body samples of white sucker were collected at four stream reaches. Smallmouth bass (*Micropterus dolomieui*) of 25- to 38-cm length were collected in 2009 and greater than 25-cm length during 2011. Smallmouth bass samples were five individual skinless fillets of at least 5 g. All fish samples were rinsed with deionized water, wrapped in plastic wrap, placed in ziplock bags, and frozen. Crayfish were collected by trapping or electroshocking. Two composites of 5 to 10 whole crayfish (more than 100 g wet weight) were collected at each site during August 2009, and 10 individual whole crayfish were collected at each site during August 2011 (Nobis Engineering, 2009). Crayfish were rinsed with deionized water, placed in a ziploc bag, and immediately chilled on wet ice.

Bats and Birds

Blood and fur from little brown bats (*Myotis lucifugus*) and big brown bats (*Eptesicus fuscus*) were sampled by BioDiversity Research Institute at the AR1 reference site (Pontook Reservoir) and downstream at AR9. Bats were collected using mist nets as described by Buck and Evers (2011). Tree swallows (*Tachycineta bicolor*) were sampled by ESAT at the two reference locations (Pontook Reservoir (AR1) and Wheeler Bay (AR2)) and four downstream stream reaches (AR3, AR4, AR8, and AR9). Blood, eggs, and feathers of adult and nestling tree swallows were collected as described in the Ecological Investigation Quality Assurance Project plan (Nobis Engineering, 2011).

Laboratory Methods

The laboratory methods detailed below were conducted by the USGS Branch of Regional Research, Western Region (USGS BRR–WR) Laboratory in Menlo Park, California, and were associated with the streambed-sediment and pore-water samples collected during 2010 only. These methods reflect the key parameters discussed in detail in this report. These and all other laboratory methods are summarized in table 2 (in back of report).

Total Mercury

THg analysis was conducted on all 60 streambed-sediment samples collected during 2010. Samples were stored frozen until analysis. After thawing, sediment THg was first extracted overnight in concentrated acid (aqua regia; concentrated nitric acid (HNO_3) plus hydrochloric acid (HCl) at a 1:3 ratio), followed by the addition of the oxidant bromine monochloride (BrCl) and heating overnight at 60 degrees Celsius (°C) to ensure all the mercury was in the divalent inorganic form (Hg(II)) in accordance with standard USGS protocol (Olund and others, 2004). THg in the extract was assayed by cold vapor atomic fluorescence spectrometry (CVAFS) using a Tekran 2006 automated total mercury analyzer in accordance with USEPA method 1631 (U.S. Environmental Protection Agency, 2001b, 2002). Further details on the method are described in Marvin-DiPasquale and others (2011). Each batch of analytical samples was accompanied by the analysis of the following minimum number of quality assurance (QA) samples: one certified reference material, one matrix spike, one analytical duplicate, one field duplicate, one method blank, and calibration standards prepared from commercially certified mercuric chloride ($HgCl_2$) solution.

Pore-water samples collected for pw.THg analysis were preserved in the field with a final concentration of 0.5-percent HCl and stored refrigerated in the dark until further processing. Subsequently, the samples were initially oxidized with BrCl and similarly analyzed by CVAFS using a Tekran 2600 automated total mercury analyzer in accordance with USEPA method (U.S. Environmental Protection Agency, 2001b, 2002). Each batch of analytical samples was accompanied by the analysis of the following minimum number of QA samples: one matrix spike, one analytical duplicate, one field duplicate, one method blank, and calibration standards prepared from commercially certified $HgCl_2$ solution. For sediment and pore water, the detection limit for the THg assay is approximately 0.5 nanogram per liter (ng/L) at the level of the autoanalyzer. QA results for sediment and pore-water THg assays are detailed in appendix 1.

Methylmercury

MeHg analysis was conducted on the 15 primary streambed-sediment samples collected during 2010. Samples were stored frozen until analysis. After thawing, sediment MeHg was first extracted with a solution of 25-percent potassium hydroxide (KOH) in methanol at 60 °C for 4 hours (Xianchao and others, 2005). Quantification of MeHg in the extract was then carried out after ethylation of the analyte using a Brooks Rand Labs automated MeHg analyzer (MERX). Further method details are described in Marvin-DiPasquale and others (2011). Each batch of analytical samples was accompanied by the analysis of the following minimum number of QA samples: one certified reference material, one matrix spike, one analytical duplicate, one field duplicate, one method blank, and calibration standards prepared from commercial crystalline methylmercury chloride (MeHgCl) and compared with a separate, commercially available MeHg standard solution.

Pore-water samples collected for pw.MeHg analysis were preserved in the field with a final concentration of 0.5 percent HCl and stored refrigerated in the dark until further processing. Subsequently samples were distilled (U.S. Environmental Protection Agency, 2001b) and then quantified after ethylation of the analyte using a MERX (Marvin-DiPasquale and others, 2011). The detection limit for the MeHg assay is approximately 0.5 picogram (pg; absolute mass as mercury). QA results for sediment and pore-water MeHg assays are detailed in appendix 1.

Reactive Inorganic Mercury

$Hg(II)_R$ analysis was conducted on all 60 streambed-sediment samples collected during 2010. Sediment $Hg(II)_R$ is methodologically defined as the fraction of total Hg(II) that is readily reduced to Hg^0 by an excess of tin chloride ($SnCl_2$) over an exposure time of 15 minutes. Further method details are described in Marvin-DiPasquale and Cox (2007). Sediment subsamples for $Hg(II)_R$ were stored frozen until analysis. Each batch of analytical samples was accompanied by the analysis of the following minimum number of QA samples: one analytical duplicate, one field duplicate, four bubbler blanks, and calibration standards prepared from a commercial $HgCl_2$ stock solution. No commercially available certified reference material exists for $Hg(II)_R$ in sediment. The detection limit for the $Hg(II)_R$ assay is approximately 40 pg (absolute mass). QA results are detailed in appendix 1.

Methylmercury Production Potential and Microbial Divalent-Mercury-Methylation Rate Constant

MPP rates were assessed for the 15 primary streambed-sediment samples collected during 2010. Bulk sediment MPP rates were quantified using a stable isotope incubation approach (Marvin-DiPasquale and others, 2011). Incubations were initiated 4 to 8 days after initial field collection of the sediment. Three subsamples of sediment (3.0 g wet weight) per site were transferred into 13-cubic centimeter (cm^3) sealed serum vials under anaerobic conditions (nitrogen gas (N_2)-flushed glove bag). An isotopically enriched solution (0.1 milliliter (mL)) of mercury chloride ($^{200}HgCl_2$) was then injected through the sepum of each vial for a final amendment concentration of 38 nanograms (ng) of isotopic mercury ($^{200}Hg(II)$) per gram of sediment (wet weight). The samples were vortexed for 1 minute each immediately following the isotope amendment. One sample per set was immediately flash frozen in a bath of dry ice and ethanol. This sample represented the killed control. The remaining two samples per set were incubated at 20 °C for 5 hours, after which they too were flash frozen in dry ice and ethanol and stored at -80 °C until further processing, which consisted of extraction with 25-percent KOH in methanol and quantification by isotope-dilution inductively coupled plasma mass spectrometry (ICP–MS; Marvin-DiPasquale and others, 2011).

Pseudo-first-order rate constants for ^{200}Hg(II)-methylation (k_{meth}, units = 1/done per day) were then calculated from the incubated samples as described for the radiotracer ^{203}Hg(II)-methylation assay in Marvin-DiPasquale and others (2008).

Daily MPP rates (in ng/g dry sediment per day) were calculated as:

$$MPP = Hg(II)_R - \left(Hg(II)_R \times \exp\left(k_{meth} \times t \right) \right), \quad (1)$$

where

t is the time during which methylation occurred (for the purposes of this rate, 1 day); and

$Hg(II)_R$ is the independently measured in-situ concentration of inorganic reactive mercury, in ng/g dry weight.

QA consisted of killed controls, analytical duplicates for every site, and the use of internal standards (that is, isotopically enriched MeHg (Me^{199}Hg)).

Mercury Sequential Extraction

THg sequential extraction analysis was conducted on the 15 primary streambed-sediment samples collected during 2010. Sediment sequential extraction followed the five-fraction (F1 thru F5) scheme detailed in Bloom and others (2003) and Marvin-DiPasquale and others (2011) with each successive fraction using a stronger extraction solution (from deionized water to aqua regia) to dissolve mercury in the sediment sample. The specific extraction solutions and typical mercury species extracted with them are detailed in table 3. The starting sample mass extracted was 3 ±0.2 g wet weight with the exact weight (±0.001 g) noted. Each extraction step

was conducted overnight for a minimum of 12 hours. The analysis of THg on each extraction fraction was conducted as described above for pore water. For QA, 3 of the 15 samples were run in duplicate, as were reagent blanks for all extractants. The relative percent difference (mean plus or minus standard error) for analytical duplicates associated with the five fractions were as follows (number of samples in each case equals three): F1 = 21 ±16 percent, F2 = 30 ±6 percent, F3 = 7.5 ±3.9 percent, F4 = 22 ±14 percent, and F5 = 9.6 ±5.3 percent. No certified reference material is commercially available for these method-defined sequential extraction fractions.

Iron Speciation

Iron speciation analysis was conducted on the 15 primary streambed-sediment samples collected during 2010. Samples were stored frozen until analysis. Three forms of sediment iron were assayed: acid-extractable ferrous iron (Fe(II)$_{AE}$), amorphous (poorly crystalline) ferric iron (Fe(III)$_a$), and crystalline ferric iron (Fe(III)$_c$). Method details are described in Marvin-DiPasquale and others (2008). The typical detection limit for each iron fraction is approximately 0.01 milligram per milliliter (mg/mL) at the level of the spectrophotometric analysis. Each batch of analytical samples was accompanied by the analysis of the following minimum number of QA samples: one analytical duplicate, one field duplicate, one matrix spike for Fe(II)$_{AE}$ and Fe(III)$_c$ fractions only, one method blank, and ferrous sulfate (FeSO$_4$) calibration standards prepared from analytical-grade crystalline reagents. No certified reference material is commercially available for these method-defined iron species. QA results are detailed in appendix 1.

Total Reduced Sulfur

Total reduced sulfur (TRS) analysis was conducted on the 15 primary streambed-sediment samples collected during 2010. Samples were stored frozen until analysis. After

Table 3. Sequential extraction scheme applied to surface sediment samples from the Androscoggin River, Coos County, New Hampshire.

[The mercury sequential extraction sequence (Bloom and others, 2003) with each fraction number (F#) is described by the extraction solution used and the dominant mercury species associated with that fraction. DI, deionized; Hg, mercury; HgCl$_2$, mercuric chloride; HgSO$_4$, mercuric sulfate; M, moles per liter; HCl, hydrochloric acid; HgO, mercuric oxide; KOH, potassium hydroxide; Hg(II), inorganic divalent mercury; MeHg, methylmercury; Hg$_2$Cl$_2$, mercurous chloride; HNO$_3$, nitric acid; Hg^0, elemental mercury; HgS, cinnabar; m-HgS, metacinnabar; HgAu, mercury gold amalgam]

F#	Extraction	Dominant mercury species
F1	DI water	Soluble, HgCl$_2$, HgSO$_4$
F2	pH = 2; 0.1 M acetic acid plus 0.01 M HCl	HgO, HgSO$_4$
F3	1 M KOH	Organic or particle bound Hg(II), MeHg, Hg$_2$Cl$_2$
F4	12 M HNO$_3$	Elemental Hg^0, Hg$_2$Cl$_2$
F5	Aqua regia (concentrated HNO$_3$ and HCl at 1:3 ratio)	HgS, m-HgS, HgAu

thawing, sediment TRS was extracted by a single-step hot acid chromium reduction approach and quantified spectrophotometrically (Marvin-DiPasquale and others, 2008). Each batch of analytical samples was accompanied by the analysis of the following minimum number of QA samples: one analytical duplicate, one field duplicate, one method blank, and zinc sulfide (ZnS) calibration standards. No certified reference material is commercially available for the TRS assay. The detection limit for this assay is approximately 0.2 micromole per milliliter (μmol/mL) at the level of the spectrophotometric analysis. QA results are detailed in appendix 1.

Grain Size

Grain-size analysis was conducted on all 60 streambed-sediment samples collected during 2010. Samples were stored refrigerated until analysis. Sediment percent fines was assayed as the weight percentage of dry sediment less than 63 micrometers (less than 63 μm, the sand/silt split) and was conducted by wet sieving (Matthes and others, 1992). Each batch of analytical samples was accompanied by the analysis of the following minimum number of QA samples: one analytical duplicate and one field duplicate. No certified reference material is commercially available for the grain size analysis. QA results are detailed in appendix 1.

Dry Weight, Bulk Density, Porosity, and Organic Content

Analysis of bulk density, dry weight, porosity, and organic content (as percent LOI) was conducted on all 60 streambed-sediment samples collected during 2010. Samples were stored refrigerated until analysis. These four sediment parameters were analyzed consecutively from single sediment subsamples, as previously detailed (Marvin-DiPasquale and others, 2008). Each batch of analytical samples was accompanied by the analysis of the following minimum number of QA samples: one analytical duplicate at all sites and one field duplicate. No certified reference material is commercially available for this suite of sediment analyses. QA results are detailed in appendix 1 (table 1–3).

Total and Organic Carbon, Total Nitrogen, and Carbon and Nitrogen Isotopes

Analysis of total carbon (TC), total organic carbon (TOC), and total nitrogen (TN), with associated isotopes (δ^{13}C and δ^{15}N, respectively), was conducted on all 60 streambed-sediment samples collected during 2010. Samples were stored frozen until analysis. Analysis was conducted as described in Kendall and others (2001) using a Carlo Erba model 1500 elemental analyzer connected to an Elementar Isoprime mass spectrometer before and after acidification (HCl acid fuming overnight to remove inorganic carbon). Each batch of

analytical samples was accompanied by the analysis of the following minimum number of QA samples: one analytical duplicate, one field duplicate, and calibration standards prepared from ethylene-diamine-tetra-acetic acid. QA results for TC and TN are detailed in appendix 1.

Pore-Water Dissolved Organic Carbon

Analysis of pw.DOC was conducted on pore water collected from the 15 primary streambed sites sampled during 2010. Samples were stored refrigerated and acidified (to a pH of less than 2) until analysis. Analysis for pw.DOC was conducted using high temperature combustion and infrared (IR) detection on a Shimadzu Scientific Instruments TOC–VCPH total organic carbon analyzer. QA measures included analytical duplicates, field duplicates, calibration standards, method blanks, and reagent blanks. QA results are detailed in appendix 1.

Pore-Water Sulfate and Chloride

Analysis of pw.SO$_4$ and pore-water chloride (pw.Cl) was conducted on pore water collected from the 15 primary streambed sites sampled during 2010. Samples were stored frozen until analysis and assayed by ion chromatography as described in Marvin-DiPasquale and others (2008). QA measures included analytical duplicates, field duplicates, calibration standards, method blanks, and reagent blanks. QA results are detailed in appendix 1.

Pore-Water Ferrous Iron

Analysis of pw.Fe(II) was conducted on pore water collected from the 15 primary streambed sites sampled during 2010. Samples were stored refrigerated and acidified (to a pH of less than 2) until analysis and assayed by the colorimetric ferrozine assay as described in Marvin-DiPasquale and others (2008). QA measures included analytical duplicates, field duplicates, calibration standards, method blanks, and reagent blanks. QA results are detailed in appendix 1.

Data Analysis

Statistical analysis was performed using the TICBO Sptofire S+, version 8.1 software. Type II error probability (p) was set at less than 0.05 for all statistical tests, unless otherwise noted. We generally report median and interquartile range (IQR) data throughout the Results and Discussion section because the two-sided Kolmogorov-Smirnov goodness-of-fit test indicated that a majority (more than 60 percent) of the parameters measured in this study were not normally distributed. For data below the reporting limit, medians and IQRs were calculated using maximum likelihood estimation (Helsel, 2005) subroutines developed by the USGS for the

S+ statistical platform. The mercury distribution in sediment, pore water, and biota was analyzed by comparing grouped medians from samples collected downstream from the former chloralkali facility to the reference sites using the nonparametric Wilcoxon rank sum (WRS) test. Downstream stream reaches were split into two spatial groupings determined by stream gradient: near-stream reaches (AR3 (fish only), AR4, AR5, and AR6), 0 to 4 km downstream from the point source in an area of steep stream gradients, and far-stream reaches (AR7, AR8, and AR9), 8 to 16 km downstream from the point source where stream gradients were much more gradual (fig. 1). Grouped medians of samples collected from reference, near, and far-stream reaches were compared using the nonparametric Kruskal-Wallis rank sum (KWRS) test. If KWRS indicated a significant difference between groupings, Tukey multiple-comparison test was used to determine which medians differed significantly.

Starting with multiple (four to seven) explanatory variables, best-fit linear model equations were developed using step-wise linear regression to describe the spatial variability in key mercury metrics. Prior to model development, parameters that were not normally distributed were log-base 10 ($\log_{10}$)-transformed and used in the model. Explanatory variables (independent or x variables) with type II error p more than 0.1 were removed from the regression equations; all overall model fits required p less than 0.05 as a testing criterion.

Results and Discussion

Samples from various matrices were collected to (1) define areas of mercury contamination, (2) better understand factors controlling MeHg production and bioaccumulation, and (3) assess the ecological impact of the mercury contamination. Tabular results of all physical parameters measured and chemical analysis conducted on surface water, pore water, sediment, invertebrates, fish, bats, and birds are listed in tables A2–2 through 2–22. Sediment and pore-water analyses included in this report are only of depositional areas, not the entire stream channel. The results from the statistical (nonparametric WRS) assessment of sediment, pore water, toxicity tests, and select biota data, comparing the reference reaches (AR1 and AR2) to all stream reaches downstream from the former chloralkali plant, are summarized in table 4 (in back of report).

The results from the statistical (nonparametric KWRS) assessment of sediment, pore water, toxicity tests, and select biota data, comparing the reference reach (AR2) with near downstream stream reaches (AR3, AR4, AR5, and AR6) and with far downstream stream reaches (AR7, AR8, and AR9), are summarized in table 5 (in back of report). Ancillary parameters that showed no significant differences among the spatial groupings were not included in tables 4 or 5 (in back of report); these parameters included sediment TC, TN, carbon to nitrogen ratio (C:N), TOC, percent LOI, TRS, Fe(II)$_{AE}$,

Fe(III)$_a$, Fe(III)$_c$, carbon 13 (^{13}C) and nitrogen 15 (^{15}N) isotopes, and pore-water parameters pw.Fe(II), pw.SO$_4$, and pw.DOC. The lack of significant spatial differences generally reflected the limited range of parameter concentrations in the study area.

Mercury Speciation and Distribution

THg and MeHg concentrations in surface water, sediment, pore water, and biota were compared downstream from the former chloralkali facility relative to reference sites. Sequential extraction of surface sediment was used to assess differences in mercury speciation upstream and downstream from the facility.

Surface Water

The number (n) of observations associated with the 2009 surface-water samples was too small (n=5) for statistical evaluation of the spatial groupings used for sediment. However, visual inspection of the data (table 2–2) showed little difference among the various stream reaches sampled for filtered THg (range from 0.70 to 1.00 ng/L, mean of 0.87 ng/L), nonfiltered THg (range from 0.44 to 2.17 ng/L, mean of 1.13 ng/L), filtered MeHg (all less than 0.1 ng/L), nonfiltered MeHg (all less than 0.1 ng/L), and 1M KOH-extractable Hg(II) (all less than 0.08 ng/L). This observed limited variability between surface-water samples collected around a point source in a high-gradient stream is not surprising because of the short hydrologic residence time.

Sediment and Pore Water

Sediment THg and MeHg concentrations were significantly higher downstream from the point source than at the reference site (table 4, in back of report). The highest median sediment THg and MeHg concentrations were in stream reach AR5, 2.5 km downstream from the point source (figs. 3A and B). No significant difference existed between near- and far-stream reaches, suggesting that sediment THg and MeHg concentrations were not decreasing downstream from the point source as far as Shelburne Dam, and could possibly continue at elevated levels downstream from Shelburne Dam (table 5, in back of report).

Whereas pw.MeHg concentrations were significantly higher downstream from the point source than at the reference site, pw.THg concentrations were not (table 4, in back of report). The highest pw.THg and pw.MeHg concentrations were in stream reach AR4, 2 km downstream from the point source (figs. 4A and B). Samples from AR4 were collected in a depositional area in and around a dense stand of aquatic emergent vegetation. The median pw.DOC concentrations at this location were also three times higher than other stream reaches (fig. 5). The elevated pw.DOC concentrations at AR4 may facilitate the desorption of organic and inorganic mercury

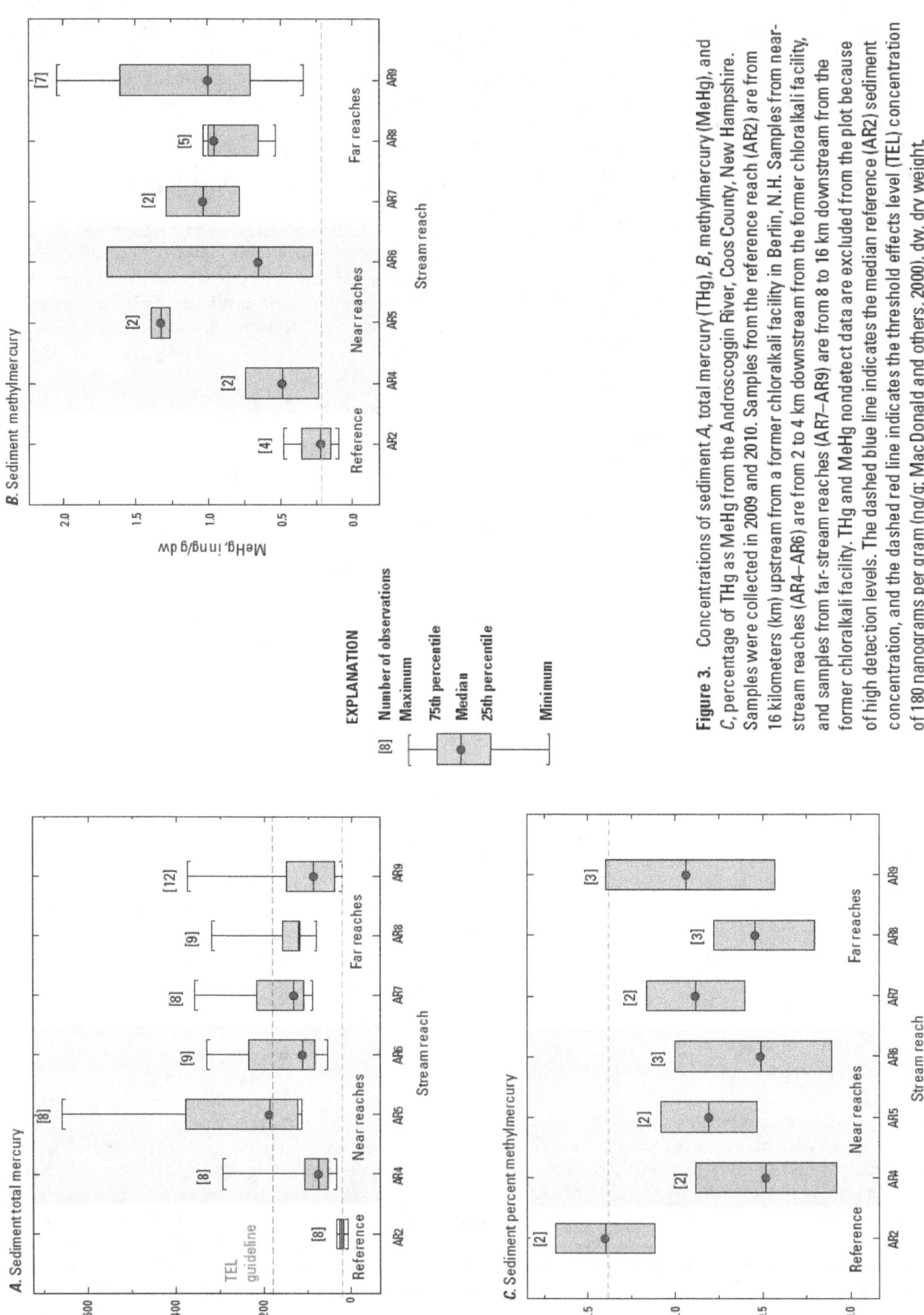

Figure 3. Concentrations of sediment *A*, total mercury (THg), *B*, methylmercury (MeHg), and *C*, percentage of THg as MeHg from the Androscoggin River, Coos County, New Hampshire. Samples were collected in 2009 and 2010. Samples from the reference reach (AR2) are from 16 kilometers (km) upstream from a former chloralkali facility in Berlin, N.H. Samples from near-stream reaches (AR4–AR6) are from 2 to 4 km downstream from the former chloralkali facility, and samples from far-stream reaches (AR7–AR9) are from 8 to 16 km downstream from the former chloralkali facility. THg and MeHg nondetect data are excluded from the plot because of high detection levels. The dashed blue line indicates the median reference (AR2) sediment concentration, and the dashed red line indicates the threshold effects level (TEL) concentration of 180 nanograms per gram (ng/g; MacDonald and others, 2000). dw, dry weight.

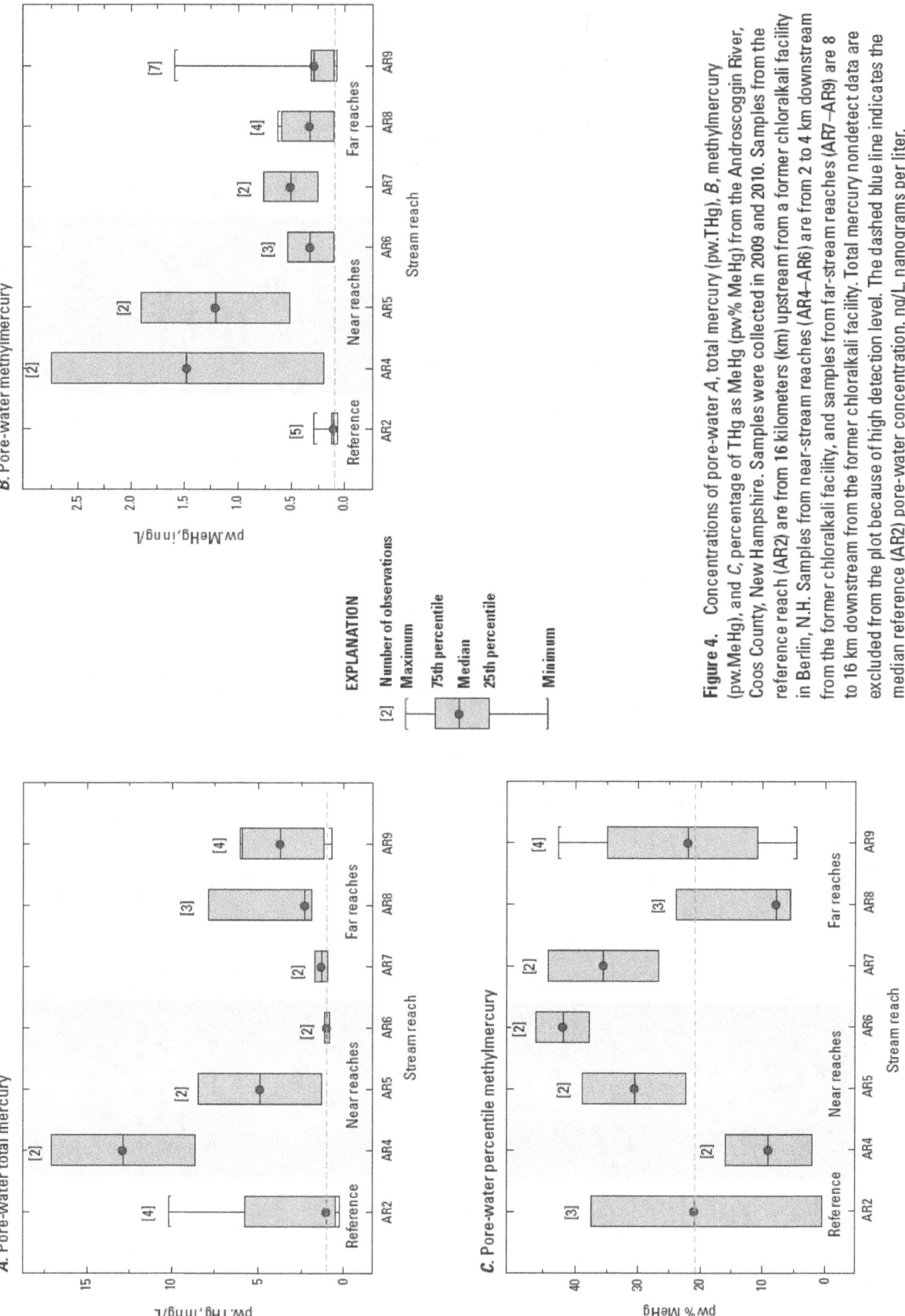

Figure 4. Concentrations of pore-water *A*, total mercury (pw.THg), *B*, methylmercury (pw.MeHg), and *C*, percentage of THg as MeHg (pw% MeHg) from the Androscoggin River, Coos County, New Hampshire. Samples were collected in 2009 and 2010. Samples from the reference reach (AR2) are from 16 kilometers (km) upstream from a former chloralkali facility in Berlin, N.H. Samples from near-stream reaches (AR4–AR6) are from 2 to 4 km downstream from the former chloralkali facility, and samples from far-stream reaches (AR7–AR9) are 8 to 16 km downstream from the former chloralkali facility. Total mercury nondetect data are excluded from the plot because of high detection level. The dashed blue line indicates the median reference (AR2) pore-water concentration. ng/L, nanograms per liter.

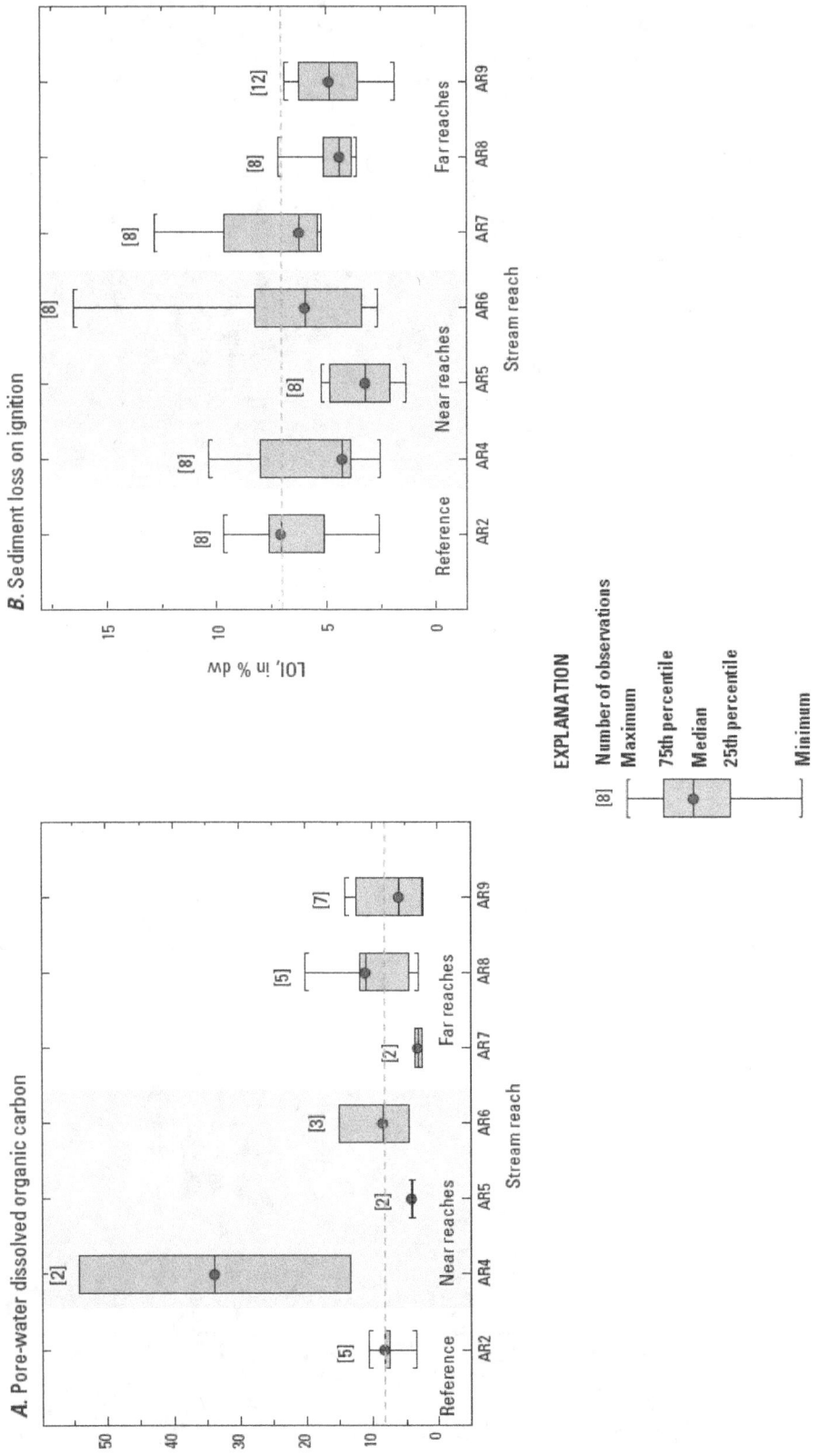

Figure 5. Concentrations of *A*, dissolved organic carbon (pw.DOC) and *B*, sediment loss on ignition (LOI) from the Androscoggin River, Coos County, New Hampshire. Samples were collected in 2009 and 2010 for pw.DOC and in 2010 for LOI. Samples from the reference reach (AR2) are from 16 kilometers (km) upstream from a former chloralkali facility in Berlin, N.H. Samples from near-stream reaches (AR4–AR6) are from 2 to 4 km downstream from the former chloralkali facility, and samples from far-stream reaches (AR7–AR9) are from 8 to 16 km downstream from the former chloralkali facility. Dashed blue line is median reference (AR2) pore-water (DOC) and sediment (LOI) concentration. dw, dry weight; mg/L, milligrams per liter; %, percent.

species off particles and into the pore water dissolved phase (Hill and others, 2009; Dong and others, 2010). The lower sediment partitioning coefficients (K_d^s) at AR4 confirmed that THg and MeHg partitioned into the dissolved phase to a greater extent in this particular reach compared with all other stream reaches (figs. 6A and B).

The distribution of mercury species as identified in surficial-sediment sequential extractions was also significantly different between the reference site and downstream from the point source (tables 4, 6, in back of report). Concentrations of the three refractory fractions (F3, F4 and F5; table 3) were all significantly higher downstream from the point source, compared with the reference site. The highest concentration of 12M HNO_3-extractable mercury (F4 fraction typified by Hg^0 or mercurous chloride (Hg_2Cl_2)) was found at AR4, the first reach downstream from the point source. At all sites, only a minor percentage (less than 0.1 percent) of THg existed in chemically labile forms (fractions F1 and F2; table 3). The relative composition of mercury species also changed downstream from the point source. The reference site had greater than 86 percent of THg in the KOH fraction, consistent with organic or particle bound Hg(II) (table 3), whereas downstream from the point source, the percentage of the F4 fraction increased dramatically (fig. 7). As much as 86 percent of the THg was found in this F4 fraction in stream reach AR4. No significant change in mercury species distribution was noted between near and far-stream reaches (table 5, in back of report), suggesting the elevated levels of refractory mercury species (potentially Hg^0 or Hg_2Cl_2) continues at least as far as Shelburne Dam.

Biota

THg concentrations in smallmouth bass, white sucker, crayfish, oligochaetes, bat fur, nestling tree swallow blood and feathers, adult tree swallow blood, and tree swallow eggs were all significantly higher downstream from the point source than at the reference sites (table 4, in back of report). Far-stream reaches had significantly higher smallmouth bass and white sucker THg concentrations than near-stream reaches (fig. 8; table 5, in back of report). Median THg concentrations in bat blood and adult swallow feathers were higher downstream from the point source than the reference site, but the difference was not significant. The highest THg concentrations in epifaunal macroinvertebrates were found in the stream reach adjacent to the point source (AR3); however, the sample size (n=5) was too small to conduct a statistical spatial comparison (table 2–16).

Smallmouth bass THg concentrations from this study were also compared with smallmouth bass fillet concentrations collected from the Androscoggin River between Rumford and Lisbon, Maine, (80–180 km downstream from the study area) by the Maine Department of Environmental Protection from 2000 to 2009 as part of the Surface Water Ambient Toxic Monitoring Program (Maine Department of Environmental Protection, 2009). Grouped medians from reference, near, far,

and Maine stream reaches were compared using nonparameteric KWRS test. Smallmouth bass THg concentrations from Maine were significantly higher than the New Hampshire reference site in Wheeler Bay (AR2) and similar to far-stream reaches (AR7–AR9) between Gorham and Shelburne, suggesting elevated THg levels in smallmouth bass continue downstream from the study area (fig. 9).

Mercury Bioavailability

The potential for Hg(II)-methylation was evaluated using a number of different metrics including the percentage of THg as MeHg (percent MeHg) in sediment, tin-reducible inorganic mercury (Hg(II)$_R$), stable isotope ^{200}Hg(II)-methylation rate incubations to derive k_{meth}, MPP rates calculated from independently measured k_{meth} and Hg(II)$_R$ data, and THg sequential extraction. Selective sequential extractions measured how readily mercury was leached from sediment; more readily leached organic bound mercury species are presumably more bioavailable for Hg(II)-methylation than the more refractory (strong acid soluble) compounds. All metrics indicated that mercury was relatively more available for Hg(II)-methylation at the reference site than downstream from the point source. The sediment percent Hg(II)$_R$ was significantly higher at the reference site than downstream from the point source (fig. 10B; table 4, in back of report). The median percent MeHg in sediment was highest at the reference site (fig. 3C); however, the difference was not significant, most likely due to the limited number of samples from the reference site (table 4, in back of report). Sequential extraction results indicated that a significantly higher percentage of THg was associated with the F3 fraction (KOH soluble, indicative of organic or particle bound mercury) at the reference site, whereas sites downstream from the point source had a significantly higher percentage of refractory forms (F4 and F5 fractions; fig. 7; table 4, in back of report).

Although the proportion of mercury readily available for Hg(II)-methylation appeared greater at the reference site compared with stream reaches downstream from the point source, the absolute concentration of Hg(II) readily available for Hg(II)-methylation and the extent of mercury bioaccumulation in biota was greater downstream from the point source. Sediment Hg(II)$_R$ concentrations were significantly higher downstream from the point source than at the reference site, as were THg concentrations in smallmouth bass, white sucker, crayfish, oligochaetes, bat fur, and swallow feathers, blood, and eggs (figs. 10A, 8A and B; table 4, in back of report). Sequential extractions of surficial sediment also indicated significantly higher concentrations of organic or particle bound mercury (F3 fraction) downstream from the point source compared with the reference site (table 4, in back of report). Median values for MPP and k_{meth} were also higher downstream from the point source compared with the reference site, but the difference was not significant most likely due to the small number of observations (n=2) at the

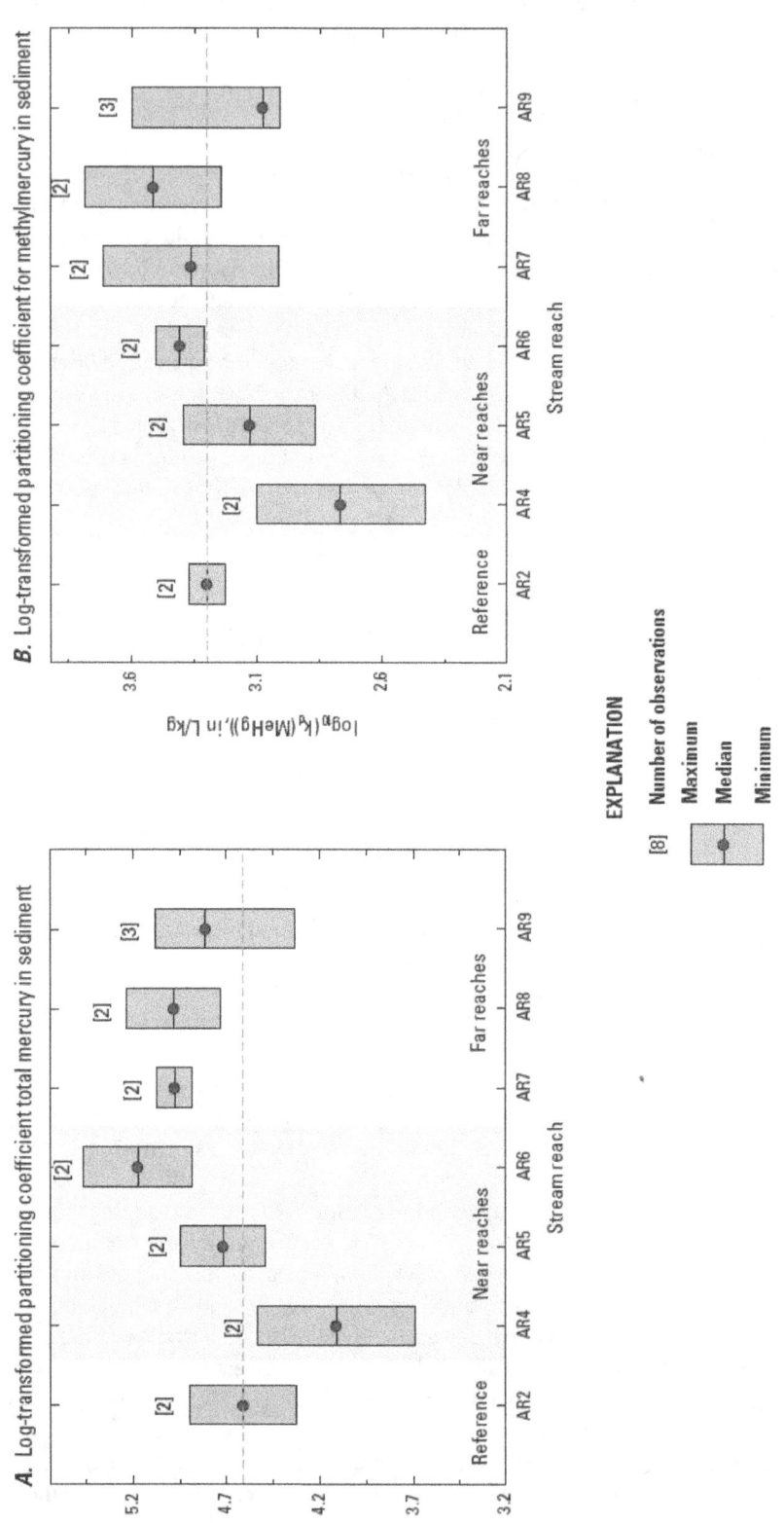

Figure 6. Mercury partitioning coefficients from the Androscoggin River, Coos County, New Hampshire. Samples were collected in 2010. Samples from the reference reach (AR2) are from 16 kilometers (km) upstream from a former chloralkali facility in Berlin, N.H. Samples from near-stream reaches (AR4–AR6) are from 2 to 4 km downstream from the former chloralkali facility, and samples from far-stream reaches (AR7–AR9) are from 8 to 16 km downstream from the former chloralkali facility. Dashed blue line is median reference (AR2) partitioning coefficient for total mercury (k_d(THg)), and partitioning coefficient for methylmercury (k_d(MeHg)). L/kg, liters per kilogram; $\log_{10}$, base-10 logarithm.

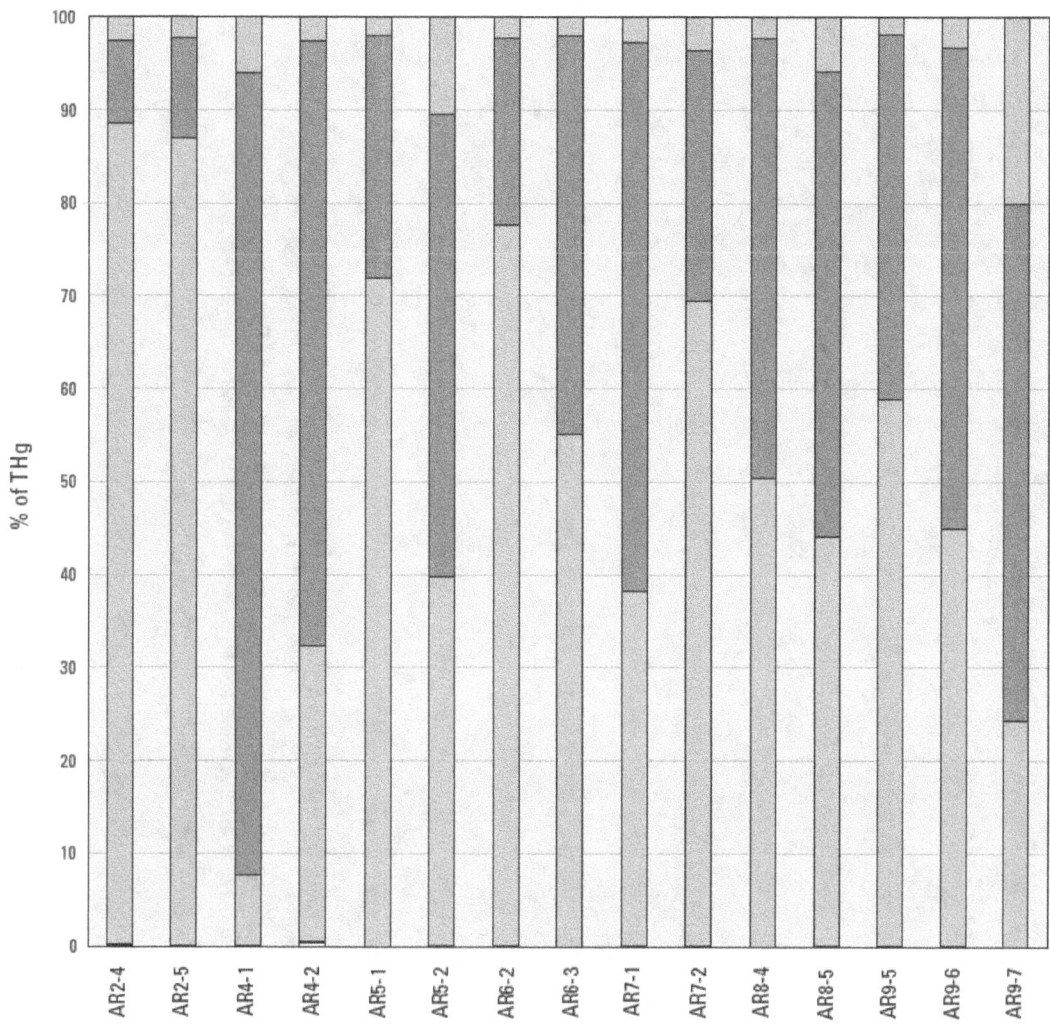

Figure 7. Sequential extractions of surficial sediment in the Androscoggin River, Coos County, New Hampshire. The mercury sequential extraction sequence (Bloom and others, 2003) shows each fraction number (F#) described by both the extraction solution used and the dominant mercury species associated with that fraction. AR, Androscoggin River, shows reach and site number (for example, AR2–4 is reach 2, site 4); Hg^0, elemental mercury; Hg(II), divalent inorganic mercury; HgAu, mercury and gold amalgam; $HgCl_2$, mercuric chloride; Hg_2Cl_2, mercurous chloride; HgO, mercuric oxide; HgS, cinnabar; $HgSO_4$, mercuric sulfate; HNO_3, nitric acid; KOH, potassium hydroxide; M, moles per liter; MeHg, methylmercury; m-HgS, metacinnabar; % of THg, percentage of total mercury as fraction number (F#).

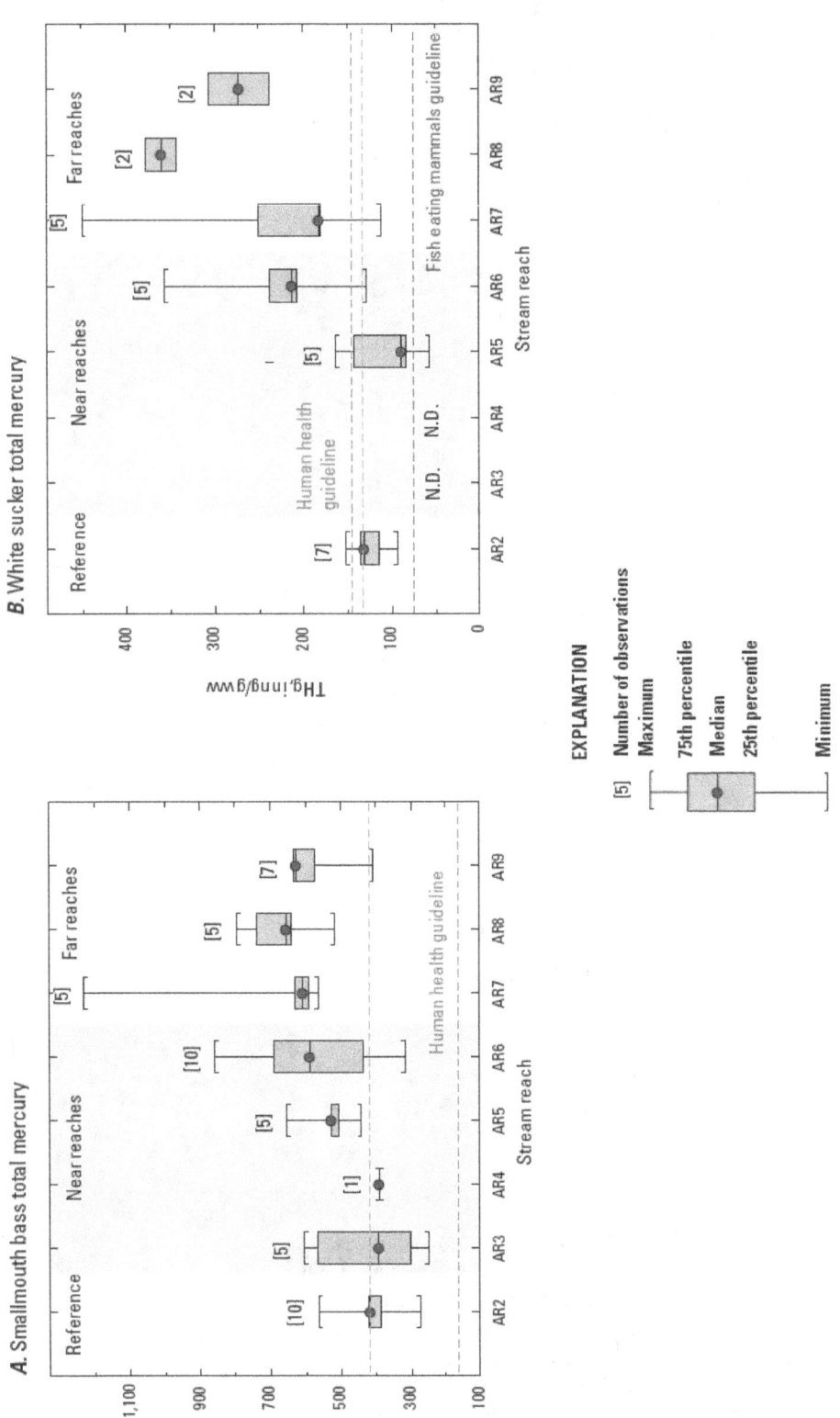

Figure 8.   Concentrations of total mercury (THg) in *A*, smallmouth bass and *B*, white sucker from the Androscoggin River, Coos County, New Hampshire. Smallmouth bass samples are skin-off fillets; white sucker samples are whole fish. Samples were collected in 2009 and 2011. Stream reaches are signified by AR followed by number. The dashed blue line is the median reference (AR2) fish tissue concentration. The dashed red line is U.S. Environmental Protection Agency (2001, 2010) human health guideline for concentration of methylmercury (MeHg; less than 95 percent of THg), which in fish is 140 nanograms per gram (ng/g). The purple dashed line is the fish-eating mammal (otter) guideline concentration of 79 ng/g (Sample and others, 1996). N.D., no data were collected from stream reach; ng/g, nanograms per gram; ww, wet weight.

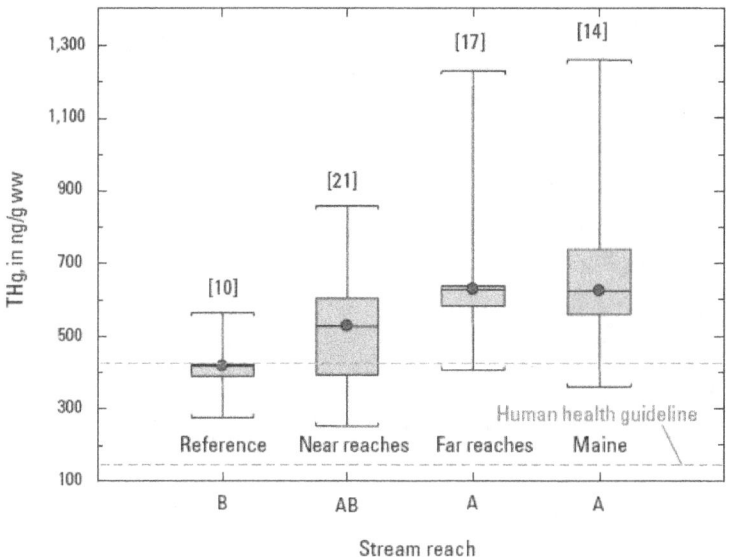
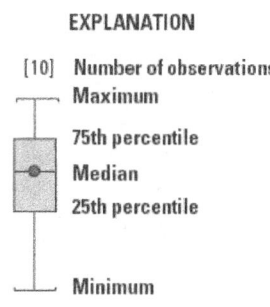

Figure 9. Concentrations of total mercury (THg) in smallmouth bass from the Androscoggin River. The reference reach is 16 kilometers (km) upstream from a former chloralkali facility in Berlin, N.H., near-stream reaches are 0 to 4 km downstream from the former chloralkali facility, far-stream reaches are 8 to 16 km downstream from the former chloralkali facility in Gorham and Shelburne, N.H., and the Maine sampling reach is 80 to 180 km downstream from the former chloralkali facility (Rumford to Lisbon, Maine). Data from Maine were collected by the Maine Department of Environmental Protection Surface Water Ambient Toxics Monitoring Program from 1990 through 2009. Data for New Hampshire were collected between 2009 and 2011. The dashed blue line is median reference (AR2) fish tissue concentration; red dashed line is the U.S. Environmental Protection Agency (2001, 2009) human health guideline. Letters A, B, and AB indicate statistical significance: Stream reaches labeled with "A" are statistically different than stream reaches labeled with "B", and stream reaches labeled "AB" are not statistically different than stream reaches labeled "A" or "B." ng/g, nanograms per gram; ww, wet weight.

reference site (table 4, in back of report). The highest values of k_{meth} were observed at AR4 (fig. 10C), an observation that was likely driven by the high concentrations of pw.SO_4 and pw.DOC fueling sulfate-reducing Hg(II)-methylating microbial activity and consistent with the high sediment TRS concentrations and low sediment oxidation reduction potential (also known as redox; E_h) also observed at this site (figs. 5, 11, and 12B). The highest calculated MPP rates were at stream reaches AR4 and AR7 (fig. 10D). Interestingly, the elevated MPP rates at AR4 were driven by the high k_{meth} values, whereas the elevated MPP rates at AR7 were driven by high $Hg(II)_R$ concentrations (fig. 10A).

Not only was the absolute concentration of $Hg(II)_R$ greater downstream from the point source than at the reference site, but the concentration generally increased with distance downstream from the point source (fig. 10A). Far sites (8 to 16 km downstream from the point source) had significantly higher $Hg(II)_R$ concentrations in whole sediment than near sites (table 5, in back of report). Similarly, the bioaccumulation of mercury generally increased with distance downstream

from the point source. THg concentrations in smallmouth bass and white sucker were significantly higher in far-stream reaches than near-stream reaches (table 5, in back of report). Near-stream reaches are comparatively short and have a high gradient, whereas far-stream reaches are longer and lower in gradient (fig. 1). The longer, lower gradient far-stream reaches appear to have conditions more conducive to methylation than the high-gradient near-stream reaches, which may reflect a difference in the type and size of particles that are likely to be deposited in these two contrasting hydrologic settings and the effect that particles have on the speciation and availability of mercury deposited to the benthos.

Controls on Mercury Distribution

Using step-wise linear regression and beginning with potential explanatory variables of sediment organic carbon (measured as percent LOI), bulk density (BD), percent fines, and percent dry weight, the best single model of sediment

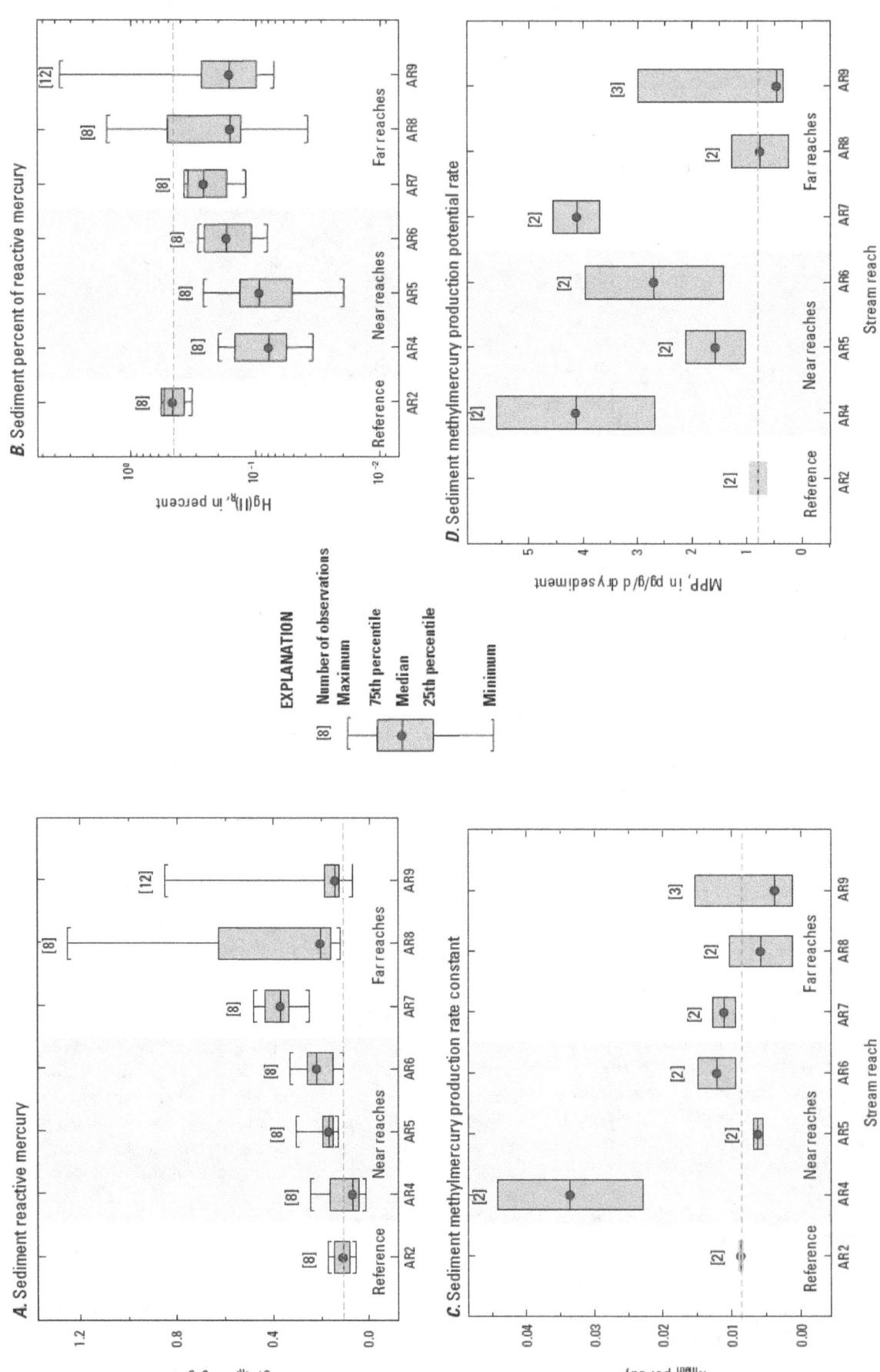

Figure 10. Sediment mercury methylation potential from the Androscoggin River, Coos County, New Hampshire. *A*, Inorganic reactive mercury (Hg(II)$_R$). *B*, Sediment percentage of THg as Hg(II)$_R$. *C*, Methylmercury production rate constant (k$_{meth}$). *D*, Methylmercury production potential (MPP) rate based on Hg(II)$_R$. Samples were collected in 2010. Samples from the reference reach (AR2) are 16 kilometers (km) upstream from a former chloralkali facility in Berlin, N.H. Samples from near-stream reaches (AR4–AR6) are 2 to 4 km downstream from the former chloralkali facility, and samples from far-stream reaches (AR7–AR9) are 8 to 16 km downstream from the former chloralkali facility. The dashed blue line is the median reference (AR2) for sediment Hg(II)$_R$ concentration (A), sediment percentage of THg as Hg(II)$_R$ (B), rate constant (C), or potential rate (D). dw, dry weight; ng/g, nanograms per gram; pg/g/d, picograms per gram per day.

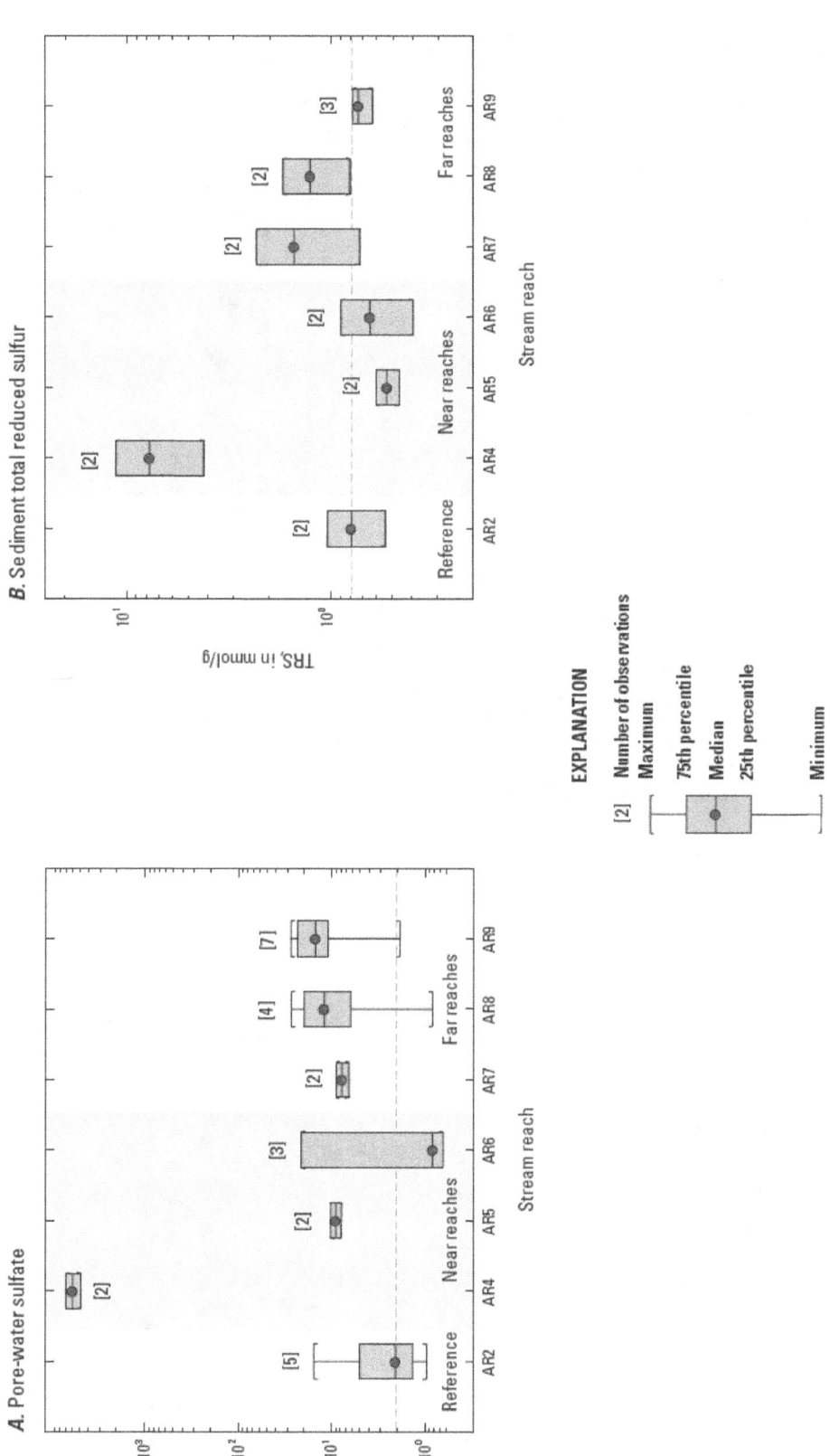

Figure 11. Concentrations of *A,* pore-water sulfate ($pw.SO_4^{-2}$) and *B,* sediment total reduced sulfur (TRS) from the Androscoggin River, Coos County, New Hampshire. Samples for $pw.SO_4^{-2}$ were collected in 2009 and 2010, and for TRS, in 2010. Samples from the reference reach (AR2) are 16 kilometers (km) upstream from a former chloralkali facility in Berlin, N.H. Samples from near-stream reaches (AR4–R6) are 2 to 4 km downstream from the former chloralkali facility, and samples from far-stream reaches (AR7–R9) are 8 to 16 km downstream from the former chloralkali facility. The dashed blue line is the median reference (AR2) pore-water (sulfate) or sediment (TRS) concentration. mg/L, milligrams per liter; mmol/g, micromoles per gram.

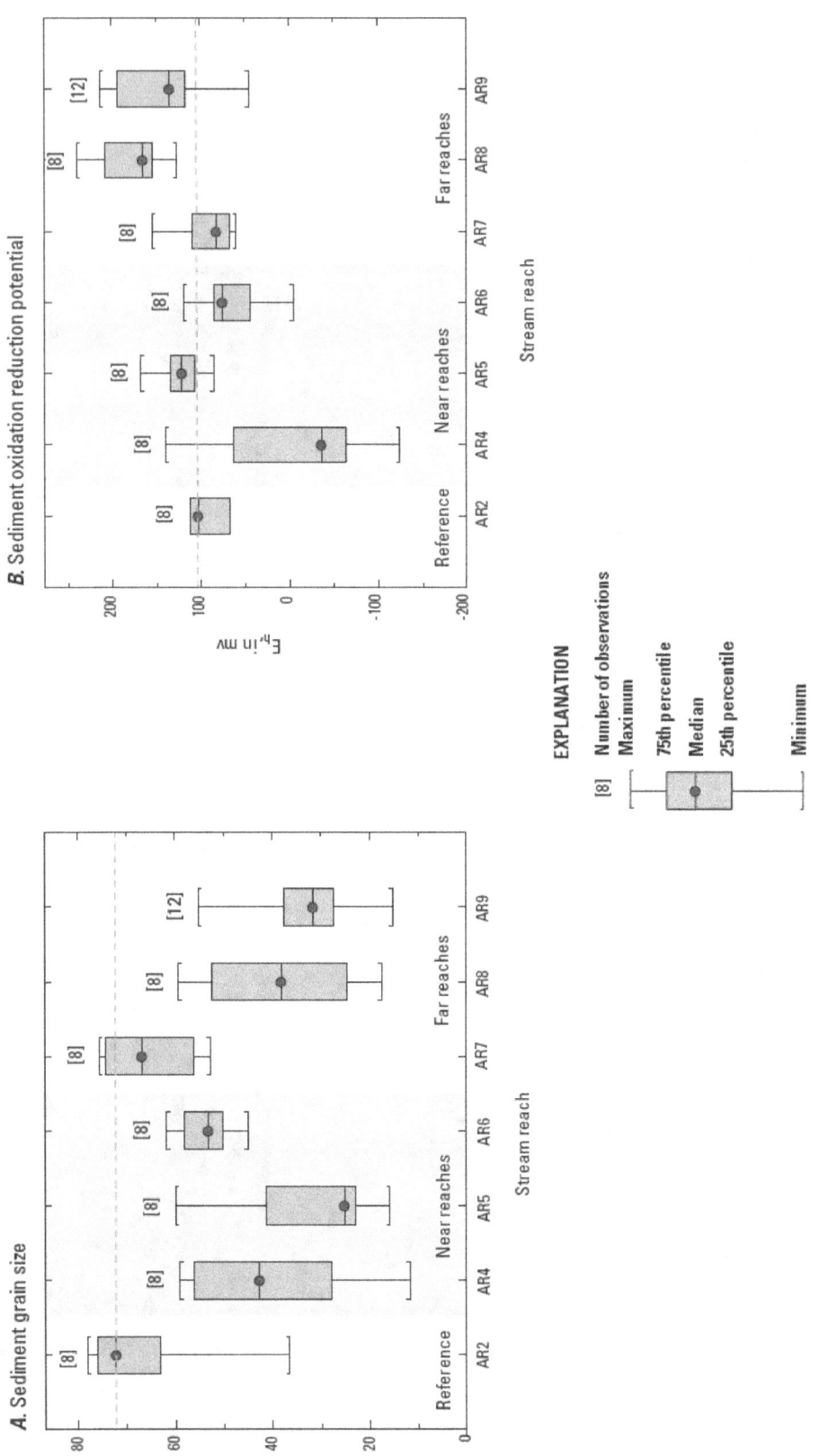

Figure 12.   *A*, Sediment grain size less than 63 micrometers (µm) and *B*, oxidation reduction potential (redox, E$_h$) from the Androscoggin River, Coos County, New Hampshire. Samples were collected in 2010. Samples from the reference reach (AR2) are 16 kilometers (km) upstream from a former chloralkali facility in Berlin, N.H. Samples from near-stream reaches (AR4–R6) are 2 to 4 km downstream from the former chloralkali facility, and samples from far-stream reaches (AR7–R9) are 8 to 16 km downstream from the former chloralkali facility. The dashed blue line is the median reference (AR2) for sediment percent grain size less than 63 micrometers (A) or sediment E$_h$ (B). mv, millivolt.

THg concentration throughout the whole study area included only percent LOI and BD, although it had low explanatory power (coefficient of determination (R^2) of 0.19). However, by grouping the downstream study area into near (AR4, AR5, and AR6) and far (AR7, AR8, and AR9) stream reaches, regression models could explain 49 to 55 percent of the variability in THg concentration (fig. 13). In the far-stream reaches, percent LOI alone explained 49 percent of the variability in sediment THg concentration. A positive relation between THg and percent LOI has been observed in a number of other studies (Hammerschmidt and Fitzgerald, 2006; Han and others, 2007; Marvin-DiPasquale and others, 2009a, b). In the higher gradient near-stream reaches, sediment BD became an important explanatory variable in addition to percent LOI, alluding to the nature of the particles that are likely to be deposited in the high-gradient environment.

Sediment MeHg concentration across all stream reaches was best described as a positive function of sediment THg concentration and a negative function of sediment TRS concentration (fig. 14), when starting with THg, $Hg(II)_R$, k_{meth}, E_h, percent LOI, TRS, and percent fines as initial explanatory variables in the stepwise regression. Sediment MeHg and THg are often correlated at lower THg concentrations (Krabbenhoft and others, 1999; Kamman and others, 2005b; Marvin-DiPasquale and others, 2009a; Scudder and others, 2009), as seen in this study. The negative relation between MeHg concentration and TRS concentration may reflect Hg(II) binding to solid-phase reduced sulfur compounds, thus reducing the amount of Hg(II) available for methylation (Huerta-Diaz and Morse, 1992; Marvin-DiPasquale and others, 2009a).

Controls on Divalent Mercury Availability for Methylation

Explanatory variables used in stepwise linear regression to describe controls on $Hg(II)_R$, k_{meth}, and MPP included percent LOI, TRS, E_h, percent fines, and THg concentration. The availability of sediment Hg(II) for Hg(II)-methylation, as assessed by the Hg(II)R assay, was best described as a multivariable linear function of sediment THg, percent fines, and E_h. Approximately 50 percent of the variability in sediment $Hg(II)_R$ could be explained by these three variables across all stream reaches, but 76 percent of $Hg(II)_R$ variability was accounted for in near-stream reaches alone using the same three variables (fig. 15). One-third of the variability in sediment $Hg(II)_R$ in far-stream reaches was explained by a combination of percent fines and E_h. Low variability in sediment THg concentrations appeared to make sediment THg a weak explanatory variable for sediment $Hg(II)_R$ in these stream reaches. The positive relation between sediment $Hg(II)_R$ and E_h likely reflects the binding kinetics of inorganic Hg(II) to solid-phase minerals and organics, which appear to increase under reducing conditions and decrease under more oxic conditions (Marvin-DiPasquale and Cox, 2007; Marvin-DiPasquale and others, 2009a, b). An increase in percent fines (a decrease in

sediment grain size) reflects more surface area and solid-phase binding sites for Hg(II).

The activity of the in-situ Hg(II)-methylating microbial community, as assessed by k_{meth}, was best predicted by E_h alone (R^2=0.59; fig. 16). The highest k_{meth} values were measured at the most chemically reducing site (AR4), and the lowest k_{meth} values were measured at the two most oxidized sites (AR8 and AR9; fig. 10). The importance of reducing conditions for microbial Hg(II)-methylation has been documented in Morel and others (1998).

Calculated MPP rates were best modeled as a combined positive function of THg concentration and negative function of sediment E_h. Because MPP rates are a function of both microbial activity (k_{meth}) and in-situ Hg(II) availability, controls on $Hg(II)_R$ and k_{meth} would also apply to MPP. Sediment organic carbon (as percent LOI) was less of an explanatory variable for predicting Hg(II)-methylation in this study compared with other studies (Lambertsson and Nilsson, 2006; Marvin-DiPasquale and others, 2009a), reflecting the limited range of organic carbon concentrations in the study area (fig. 5).

Controls on Partitioning between Bed Sediment and Pore Water

The distribution of inorganic Hg(II) and MeHg between sediment particles (solid-phase) and pore water affects the availability of inorganic Hg(II) and MeHg for Hg(II)-methylation and bioaccumulation, respectively. Grain size (Bloom and others, 1999) and organic content (Hammerschmidt and others, 2006; Sunderland and others, 2006) are often key factors in partitioning between pore water and sediment. Typically, partitioning of both THg and MeHg from sediment to pore water increases with increasing pw.DOC and decreasing percent fines (increasing grain size; Marvin-DiPasquale and others, 2009a). DOC contains strong mercury-binding ligands that increase mercury dissolution into pore water by stabilizing nanoparticles of compounds such as cinnabar (HgS; Slowey, 2010; Gerbig and others, 2011), whereas decreasing percent fines reduces particulate surface area and thus potential binding sites on sediments. The relation between the distribution coefficient for total mercury ($k_d[THg]$) and the ratio of pw.DOC to grain size [pw.DOC/percent fines] was first described by Marvin-DiPasquale and others (2009a) for eight diverse nonpoint-source streams across the United States (in Florida, Wisconsin, and Oregon) as part of the USGS National Water Quality Assessment Program (NAWQA) mercury topical study. The same pw.DOC/percent fines ratio explained 44 and 40 percent of the variability in the partitioning coefficients for THg and MeHg, respectively, in the Androscoggin River data (fig. 17).

Plotting the Androscoggin River data along with the NAWQA data (as $k_d[THg]$ against the pw.DOC/percent fines ratio; both log-base-10-transformed), we find that the both datasets fall along the same line but that the majority of the

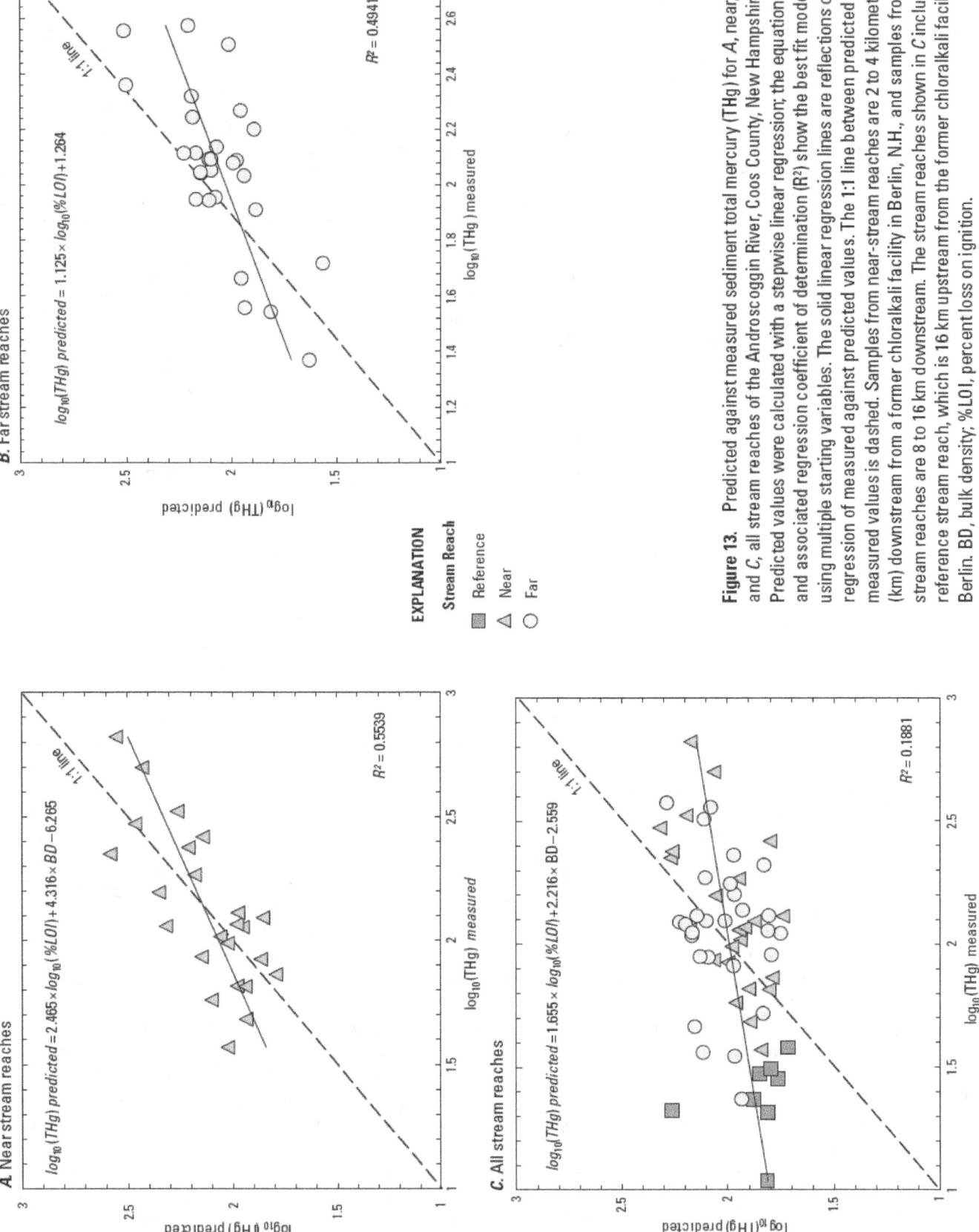

Figure 13. Predicted against measured sediment total mercury (THg) for *A*, near, *B*, far, and *C*, all stream reaches of the Androscoggin River, Coos County, New Hampshire. Predicted values were calculated with a stepwise linear regression; the equation and associated regression coefficient of determination (R^2) show the best fit model using multiple starting variables. The solid linear regression lines are reflections of the regression of measured against predicted values. The 1:1 line between predicted and measured values is dashed. Samples from near-stream reaches are 2 to 4 kilometers (km) downstream from a former chloralkali facility in Berlin, N.H., and samples from far-stream reaches are 8 to 16 km downstream. The stream reaches shown in *C* include the reference stream reach, which is 16 km upstream from the former chloralkali facility in Berlin. BD, bulk density; %LOI, percent loss on ignition.

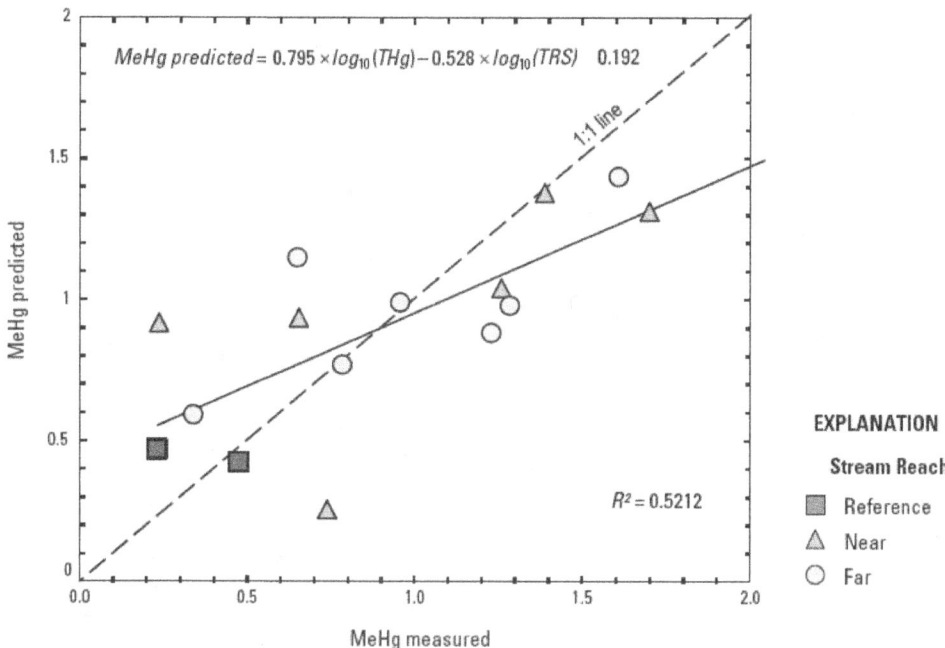

$$MeHg\ predicted = 0.795 \times log_{10}(THg) - 0.528 \times log_{10}(TRS)\quad 0.192$$

Figure 14. Predicted against measured methylmercury (MeHg) from the Androscoggin River, Coos County, New Hampshire. Predicted values were calculated with a stepwise linear regression; the equation and associated regression coefficient of determination (R^2) show the best fit model using multiple starting variables. The solid linear regression line is a reflection of the regression of measured against predicted values. The 1:1 line between predicted and measured values is dashed. Samples from the reference stream reach are 16 kilometers (km) upstream from a former chloralkali facility in Berlin, N.H. Samples from near-stream reaches are 2 to 4 km downstream from the former chloralkali facility, and samples from far-stream reaches are 8 to 16 km downstream from the former chloralkali facility. THg, total mercury; TRS, total reduced sulfur.

Androscoggin River data only occupies the upper one-third of the regression line (fig. 18). This suggests that, due to comparatively low pw.DOC or high percent fines (or some combination), THg in the Androscoggin River partitions to a greater extent onto sediment particles (larger k_d[THg] values). This would imply that THg (almost all as Hg(II)) in the samples from the Androscoggin River was comparatively less available for Hg(II)-methylation than more than one-half of the sites from the earlier NAWQA study. In contrast, MeHg partitioning coefficients (k_d[MeHg]) for the Androscoggin River fell along a parallel line to those from the NAWQA study but were generally lower for the same pw.DOC/percent fines ratio (fig. 19). This implies that MeHg in the Androscoggin River partitions to a greater extent in pore water and may be more available for bioaccumulation into the food web compared with the nonpoint source streams sampled for the NAWQA mercury study.

River-Reach Integrated Mercury Species Inventories and Methylmercury Production Potential Rates

Stream reach integrated inventories of sediment THg, Hg(II)$_R$, and MeHg, as well as MPP rates, were calculated for each stream reach sampled during 2010. These calculations were based on stream reach-specific parameters (table 7), including total stream reach area, %fine substrate (percentage of stream reach area with grain size less than 63 micrometers), stream reach-specific sediment percent dry weight (median from all samples collected for mercury analysis), stream reach-specific sediment bulk density (median from all samples collected for mercury analysis), and depth of fine substrate, as assessed with ground-penetrating radar (Degnan and others, 2011) in combination with a nonparametric analysis of the mercury species concentration data distribution (table 8),

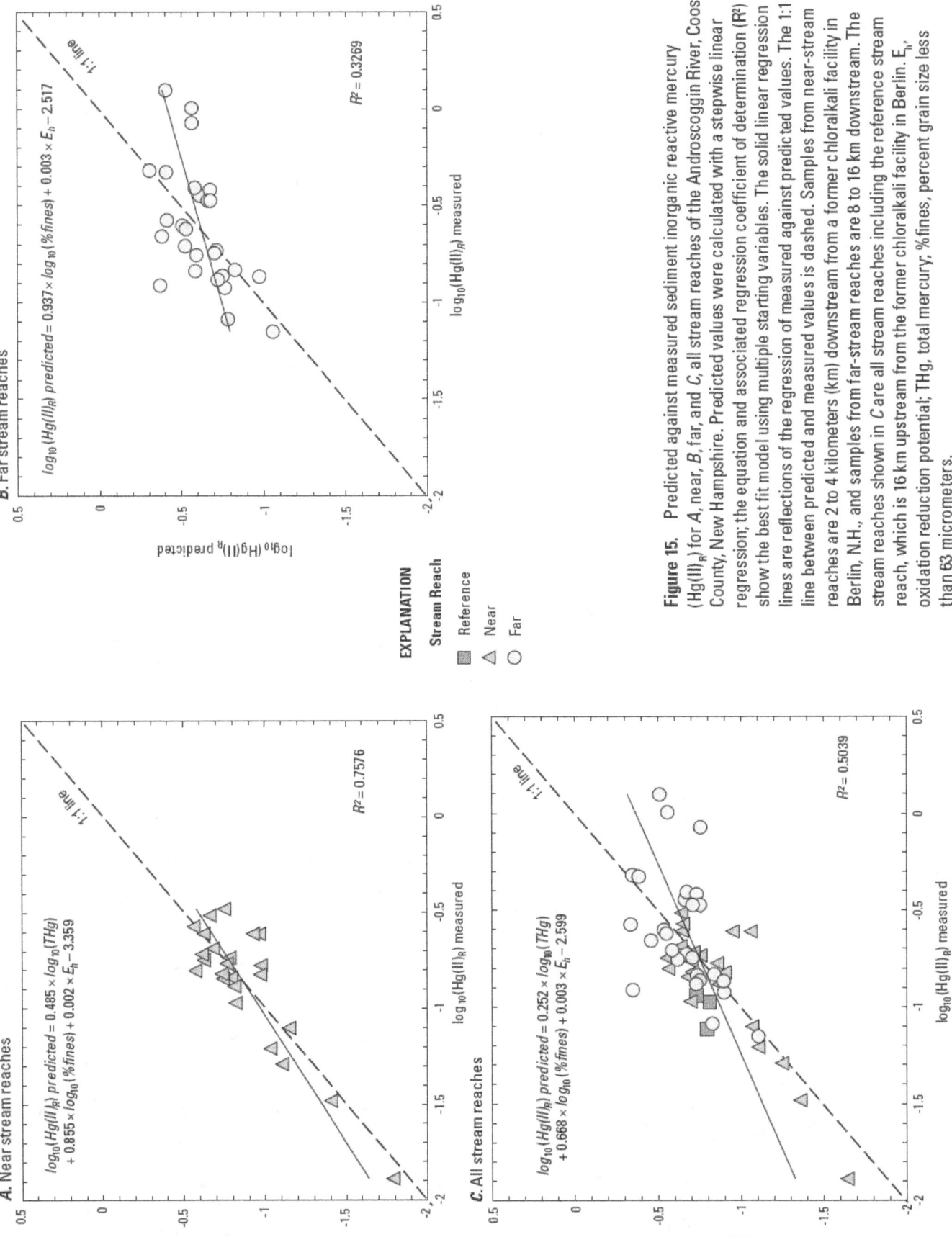

B. Far stream reaches

$log_{10}(Hg(II)_R) \; predicted = 0.937 \times log_{10}(\%fines) + 0.003 \times E_h - 2.517$

$R^2 = 0.3269$

A. Near stream reaches

$log_{10}(Hg(II)_R) \; predicted = 0.485 \times log_{10}(THg)$
$+ 0.855 \times log_{10}(\%fines) + 0.002 \times E_h - 3.359$

$R^2 = 0.7576$

C. All stream reaches

$log_{10}(Hg(II)_R) \; predicted = 0.252 \times log_{10}(THg)$
$+ 0.668 \times log_{10}(\%fines) + 0.003 \times E_h - 2.599$

$R^2 = 0.5039$

EXPLANATION

Stream Reach

Reference
Near
Far

Figure 15. Predicted against measured sediment inorganic reactive mercury $(Hg(II)_R)$ for *A*, near, *B*, far, and *C*, all stream reaches of the Androscoggin River, Coos County, New Hampshire. Predicted values were calculated with a stepwise linear regression; the equation and associated regression coefficient of determination (R^2) show the best fit model using multiple starting variables. The solid linear regression lines are reflections of the regression of measured against predicted values. The 1:1 line between predicted and measured values is dashed. Samples from near-stream reaches are 2 to 4 kilometers (km) downstream from a former chloralkali facility in Berlin, N.H., and samples from far-stream reaches are 8 to 16 km downstream. The stream reaches shown in *C* are all stream reaches including the reference stream reach, which is 16 km upstream from the former chloralkali facility in Berlin. E_h, oxidation reduction potential; THg, total mercury; %fines, percent grain size less than 63 micrometers.

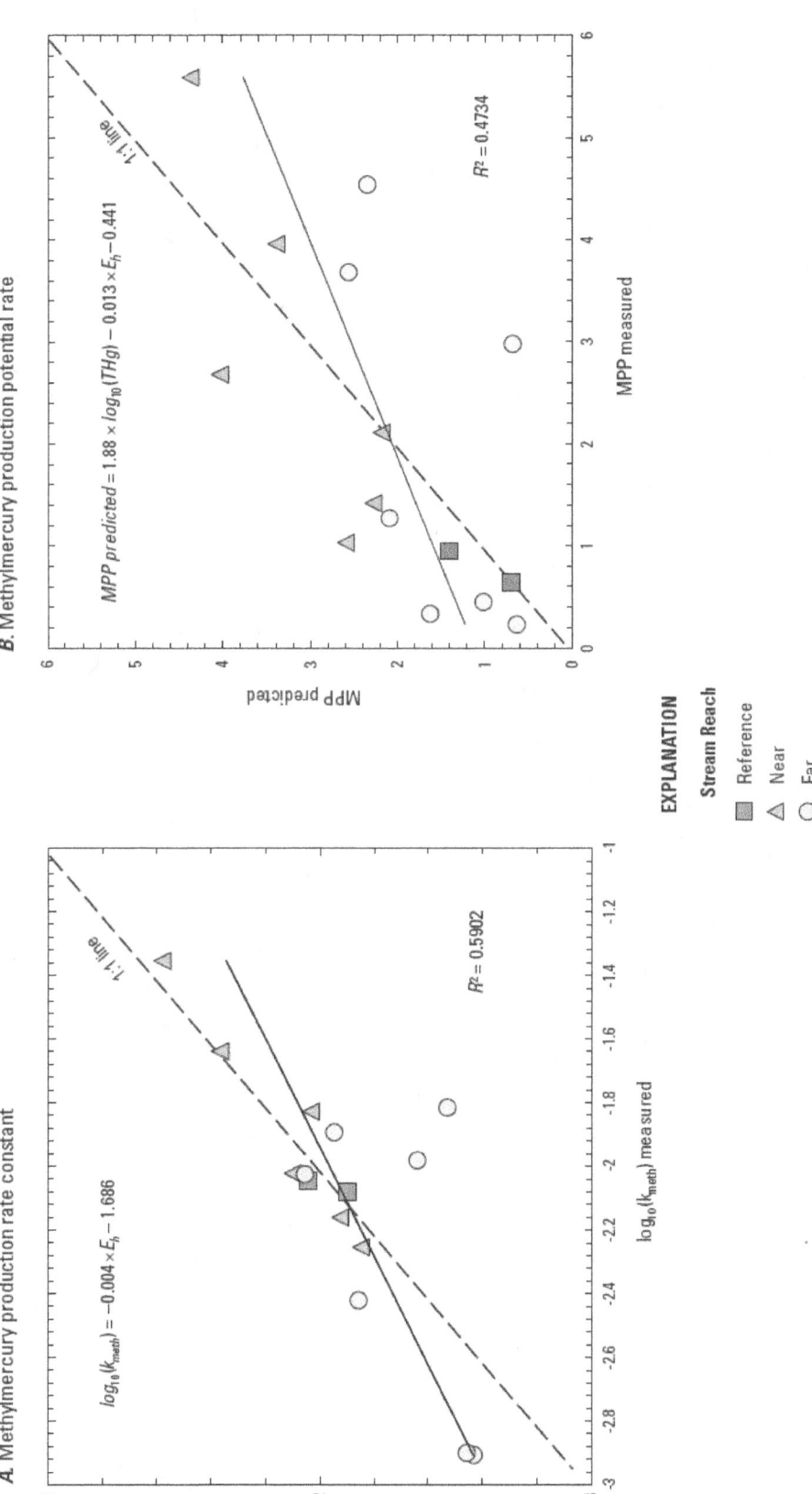

Figure 16. Predicted against measured mercury methylation potential (MPP) A, constant (k_{meth}) and B, rate for the Androscoggin River, Coos County, New Hampshire. MPP rate based on reactive mercury. Predicted values were calculated with a stepwise linear regression; the equation and associated regression coefficient of determination (R²) show the best fit model using multiple starting variables. The solid linear regression lines are reflections of the regression of measured against predicted values. The 1:1 line between predicted and measured values is dashed. Samples from the reference stream reach are 16 kilometers (km) upstream from a former chloralkali facility in Berlin, N.H. Samples from near-stream reaches are 2 to 4 km downstream from the former chloralkali facility, and samples from far-stream reaches are 8 to 16 km downstream from the former chloralkali facility. E_h, oxidation reduction potential (redox); THg, total mercury.

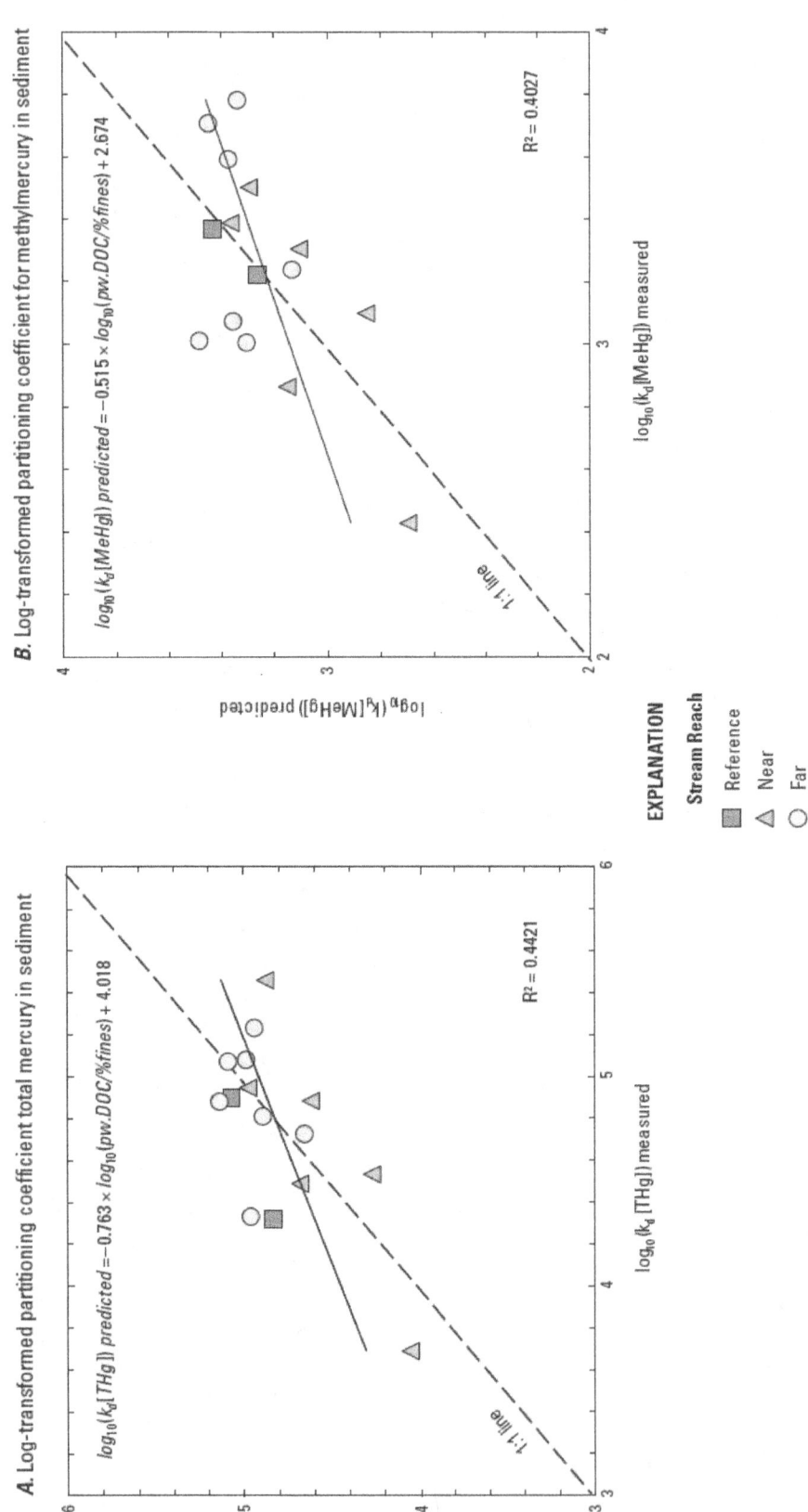

Figure 17. Predicted against measured partitioning coefficient for *A*, total mercury (k$_d$[THg]) and *B*, methylmercury (k$_d$[MeHg]) for the Androscoggin River, Coos County, New Hampshire. Predicted values were calculated with a stepwise linear regression; the equation and associated regression coefficient of determination (R^2) show the best fit model using multiple starting variables. The solid linear regression lines are reflections of the regression of measured against predicted values. The 1:1 line between predicted and measured values is dashed. Samples from the reference stream reach are 16 kilometers (km) upstream from a former chloralkali facility in Berlin, N.H. Samples from near-stream reaches are 2 to 4 km downstream from the former chloralkali facility, and samples from far-stream reaches are 8 to 16 km downstream from the former chloralkali facility. pw.DOC/%fines, ratio of pore-water dissolved organic carbon to percent grain size less than 63 micrometers.

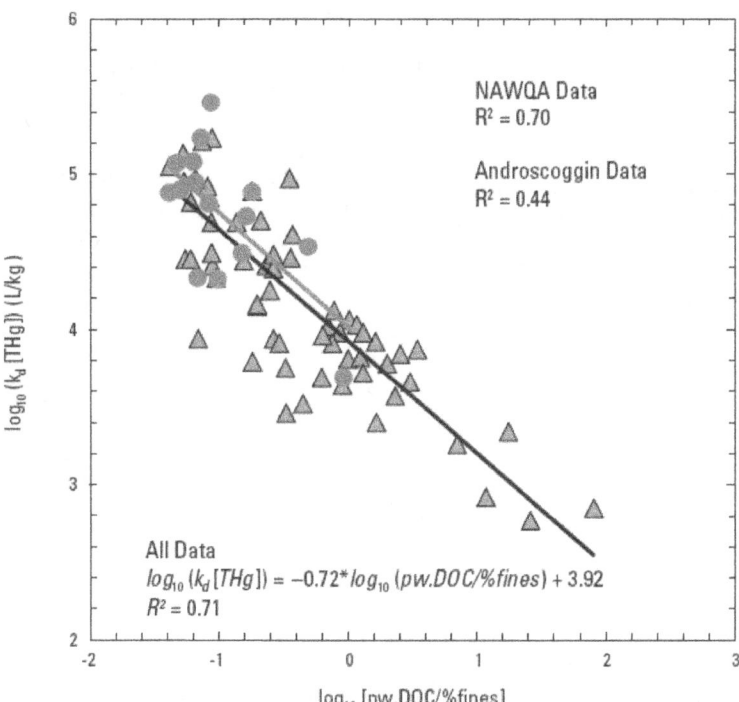

Figure 18. Sediment total mercury partitioning coefficient as a function of dissolved organic carbon and grain size. Sites on the Androscoggin River (red circles) are compared with sites sampled for the U.S. Geological Survey National Water-Quality Assessment Program (NAWQA, grey triangles) across the United States (Marvin-DiPasquale and others, 2008, 2009a). k_d [THg], sediment total mercury partitioning coefficient; L/kg, liters per kilogram; pw.DOC/%fines, ratio of dissolved organic carbon to percent grain size less than 63 micrometers; R^2, coefficient of determination]

Figure 19. Sediment methylmercury partitioning coefficient as a function of dissolved organic carbon and grain size. Sites on the Androscoggin River (red circles) are compared with sites sampled for the U.S. Geological Survey National Water-Quality Assessment Program (NAWQA, grey triangles) across the United States (Marvin-DiPasquale and others, 2008, 2009a). k_d [MeHg], sediment methylmercury partitioning coefficient; L/kg, liters per kilogram; pw.DOC/%fines, ratio of dissolved organic carbon to percent grain size less than 63 micrometers; R^2, coefficient of determination]

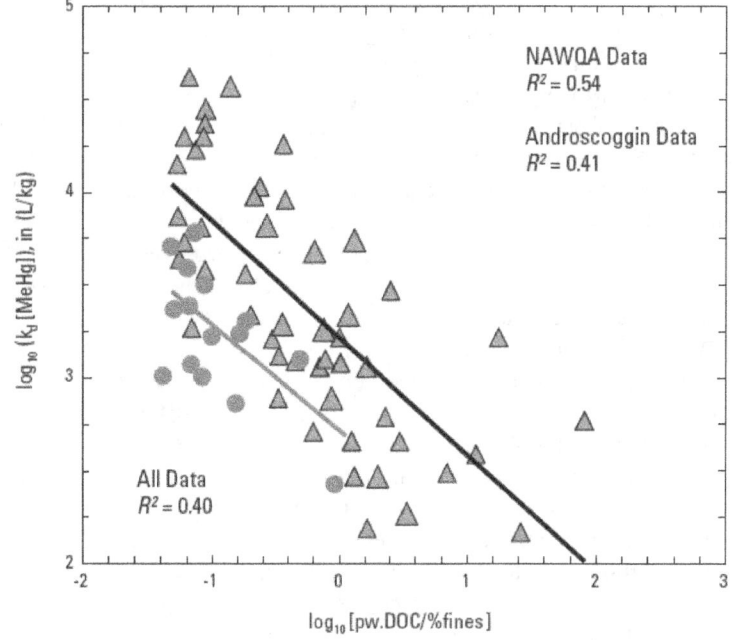

Table 7. Stream reach parameters used to calculate reach specific depth integrated mercury species inventories and rates.

[Stream reach area data are from Degnan and others (2011). Median sediment dry weight (dw) and bulk density were calculated from 2010 data only. Median depth of fine substrate was calculated excluding unknown (zero) observations. m^2, square meters; g/cm^3 ww, grams of wet weight per cubic centimeter; m, meters]

Reach	Description	Reach area, in m^2	Fine substrate, in percent of area	Median sediment, in percent dw	Median sediment bulk density, in g/cm^3 ww	Median depth of sand, silt, and clay layer, in m
AR2	Wheeler Bay	89,108	55.6	47.2	1.37	1.18
AR5	Upstream of Power Dam	53,662	10	71.7	1.73	0.95
AR7	Cascade to Brown Dam	296,807	10.5	48.2	1.37	0.79
AR9	Gorham Dam to Shelburne Dam	696,373	45.7	64.4	1.6	1.07

quartile distribution, and medians and 25 to 75 percent inter-quartile data. A simplifying assumption used in the calculation was that mercury species concentrations and MPP rates were zero for any substrate coarser than sand. Because large areas within each stream reach had substrate coarser than sand (table 7), it is likely that this simplifying assumption resulted in these inventories underestimating the actual amount of mercury species and MPP rates in each case and should be considered as minimum estimates. All mercury species inventories and MPP rates were first calculated for the top 10 cm only because that was the actual sediment sampling depth. A second simplifying assumption was that THg and $Hg(II)_R$ concentrations were constant with sediment depth. As such, we then calculated the stream reach-specific THg and $Hg(II)_R$ inventories for the full depth of the fine substrate, based on the median depth for the given reach (table 7).

Concentrations of mercury species and MPP rates, on a sediment dry weight basis, were higher in stream reaches downstream from the point source (figs. 3A, B, 10A and D; table 8). Whereas the distribution of sediment dry weight concentrations reflected the relative location of the sampling sites to the point source, stream reach-specific mercury inventories reflected the amount depositional environments with fine-grained sediment in each reach. AR9 was the largest stream reach sampled and had the largest percentage of area as fine substrate downstream from the point source (table 7). These geophysical conditions resulted in mercury inventories (total mass) being much larger in reach AR9 than in any other reach (table 8). In contrast, reach AR4 had the smallest area and the fourth smallest areal percentage of fine substrate (table 7), and as a consequence, typically had the smallest calculated mercury species inventories. For the top 0- to 10-cm-depth interval, median mercury inventory range estimates for all stream reaches downstream from the point source were as follows: THg, 0.03 to 2.91 kilograms (kg);

$Hg(II)_R$, 0.03 to 4.64 grams (g); MeHg, 0.20 to 32.9 g; and MPP rate, 1.10 to 14.8 milligrams per day (mg/d). On the basis of the median depth of the fine deposits in each reach, the median mass inventories for THg and $Hg(II)_R$ ranged from 0.21 to 31.0 kg and 0.19 to 49.4 g, respectively (table 8).

Ecological Impact

The health of the aquatic ecosystem that was potentially affected by the former chloralkali facility was evaluated using a variety of toxicity tests, biological indices, and guidelines. Results of pore-water and surface-water bioassays are detailed in Environmental Services Assistance Team (2009a, b, respectively), and bulk sediment bioassays, in EnviroSystems, Inc., (2010a, b). Survival and growth of *Hyalella azteca* and *Chironomus dilutus* in sediment and survival of *Hyalella azteca* and *Chironomus tentans* in pore water collected downstream from the former chloralkali facility were not significantly different from the reference site (table 5, in back of report). Survival and reproduction of *Ceriodaphnia dubia* and survival and growth of *Pimephales promelas* provided no evidence of toxicity of surface water collected downstream from the former chloralkali site (table 2–13; Environmental Services Assistance Team, 2009b); however, the number of samples (n=5) collected did not allow for statistical testing.

Sites were evaluated for biological condition based on scores calculated with the use of the NHDES B–IBI for invertebrate assemblages (table 2–17). The B–IBI is designed to provide a relative measure of stream health and is centered on the mean (average) value of seven indicator metrics that reflect the biological condition of streams and rivers in the region, including the Androscoggin River. The Androscoggin River reaches AR2 through AR9 were classified as being exclusive to the Hills reference sites. The 25th percentile (64.5) for

Table 8. Depth-integrated mercury species inventories and rates, by river reach.

[Mercury species and rates were calculated from 2010 data. Full depth inventories are based on median depth of fine substrate. ng/g dw, nanograms per gram dry weight; mg/m², milligrams per square meter; cm, centimeters; kg, kilograms; g, grams; Q, quartile; <, less than; %, percent]

Reach	Quartile data by reach, in ng/g dw			10-cm depth integrated, in mg/m²			Reach integrated (top 10 cm), in kg			Reach integrated (full depth), in kg		
	25th% Q	50th% Q	75th% Q	25th% Q	50th% Q	75th% Q	25th% Q	50th% Q	75th% Q	25th% Q	50th% Q	75th% Q
A. Total mercury												
AR2	21	26	30	1.3	1.7	1.9	0.07	0.08	0.10	0.78	0.97	1.70
AR4	61	79	106	5.6	7.2	9.7	0.03	0.03	0.04	0.16	0.21	0.39
AR5	128	190	321	15.9	23.6	39.9	0.09	0.13	0.21	0.81	1.21	2.44
AR6	81	106	197	7.0	9.2	17.1	0.12	0.16	0.30	1.36	1.78	4.38
AR7	112	134	214	7.4	8.8	14.1	0.23	0.27	0.44	1.82	2.17	4.80
AR8	117	123	137	12.8	13.4	15.0	0.20	0.21	0.23	1.92	2.02	3.53
AR9	44	88	137	4.5	9.1	14.1	1.43	2.91	4.50	15.3	31.0	78.6
B. Reactive inorganic mercury												
AR2	0.09	0.11	0.13	0.0055	0.0071	0.0086	0.27	0.35	0.43	3.23	4.16	7.57
AR4	0.05	0.07	0.15	0.0043	0.0065	0.0141	0.02	0.03	0.06	0.12	0.19	0.56
AR5	0.15	0.17	0.19	0.0191	0.0211	0.0236	0.1	0.11	0.13	0.98	1.08	1.44
AR6	0.15	0.22	0.25	0.0131	0.0189	0.0218	0.23	0.33	0.38	2.54	3.67	5.6
AR7	0.34	0.37	0.41	0.0222	0.0244	0.0272	0.69	0.76	0.85	5.46	6.00	9.22
AR8	0.17	0.2	0.43	0.0184	0.0222	0.0471	0.29	0.34	0.73	2.77	3.33	11.1
AR9	0.13	0.14	0.18	0.0132	0.0146	0.0187	4.21	4.64	5.94	44.8	49.4	104

Reach	Quartile data by reach, in ng/g			10-cm depth integrated, in mg/m²			Reach integrated (top 10 cm), in g		
	25th% Q	50th% Q	75th% Q	25th% Q	50th% Q	75th% Q	25th% Q	50th% Q	75th% Q
C. Methylmercury									
AR2	0.155	0.221	0.353	0.010	0.014	0.023	0.50	0.71	1.13
AR4	0.24	0.49	0.74	0.022	0.045	0.068	0.10	0.20	0.30
AR5	1.26	1.32	1.39	0.157	0.164	0.173	0.84	0.88	0.93
AR6	0.28	0.65	1.7	0.024	0.057	0.147	0.42	0.98	2.54
AR7	0.78	1.03	1.29	0.052	0.068	0.085	1.61	2.12	2.64
AR8	0.65	0.96	1	0.071	0.104	0.109	1.10	1.62	1.69
AR9	0.71	1	1.61	0.073	0.103	0.166	23.3	32.9	52.8
D. Methylmercury production potential rate									
AR2	0.00064	0.00079	0.00095	0.041	0.051	0.061	2.05	2.54	3.03
AR4	0.00268	0.00414	0.00559	0.25	0.38	0.51	1.10	1.70	2.30
AR5	0.00103	0.00157	0.00211	0.13	0.20	0.26	0.69	1.05	1.41
AR6	0.00142	0.00269	0.00396	0.12	0.23	0.34	2.12	4.02	5.92
AR7	0.00368	0.00411	0.00454	0.24	0.27	0.30	7.60	8.40	9.30
AR8	<0.00050	0.00075	0.00127	<0.054	0.082	0.14	<0.85	1.27	2.15
AR9	<0.00034	0.00045	0.00298	<0.035	0.047	0.31	<11.0	14.8	98.0

Hills reference sites is operationally defined as the threshold, and 90 percent (58) of the threshold categorizes the stream as unimpaired for the NHDES listing of impaired waters (Neils, NHDES, 2007). The B–IBI integrates the following metrics, which are denoted with (+) to indicate where values increase with improving conditions and (-) to indicate where values decrease with improving conditions:

- total taxa richness (+)

- plecoptera (stoneflies) taxa (+)

- percent chironomidae (midge) taxa (-)

- percent noninsect taxa (-)

- tolerant taxa (-)

- percent intolerant (sensitive) taxa (+)

- percent clinger taxa (+)

For (-) metrics that decrease with improving conditions, the inverse values were used in calculating the B–IBI score so that these metrics would contribute to the B–IBI increasing with improving condition. All replicates at all sites exceeded the B–IBI threshold of 58, indicating that the sites were categorized as meeting the criteria for unimpaired streams by NHDES standards (fig. 20; David Neils, NHDES, written commun., April 2011).

Jaccard's indices were used to compare species diversity within and between stream reaches. The percentage of similarity within stream reaches was 51 ±9 (average plus or minus (±) standard deviation). This compares closely to the percentage of similarity among stream reaches AR2, AR3, AR8, and AR9 (55 ±5). AR4 was the most different from other stream reaches with the percentage of similarity equal to 35 ±2. This section of the river is highly regulated, and the rock baskets were not in flowing water the entire 6.5 weeks they were in the river. Jaccard's indices did not show differences in species diversity upstream and downstream from the point source; however, Jaccard's indices did suggest flow characteristics were a major factor controlling species diversity in the study area.

Differences in total abundance, total taxa, and Ephemeroptera, Plecoptera, Trichoptera (EPT) taxa between invertebrate assemblages upstream and downstream from the point source were compared using nonparametric WRS and KWRS tests. The total abundance of organisms is a general indicator of productivity, whereas total taxa and EPT taxa are two indicators of taxonomic complexity in the assemblages. The highest total abundance occurred at AR3 adjacent to the former chloralkali facility (table 2–17). The higher abundance

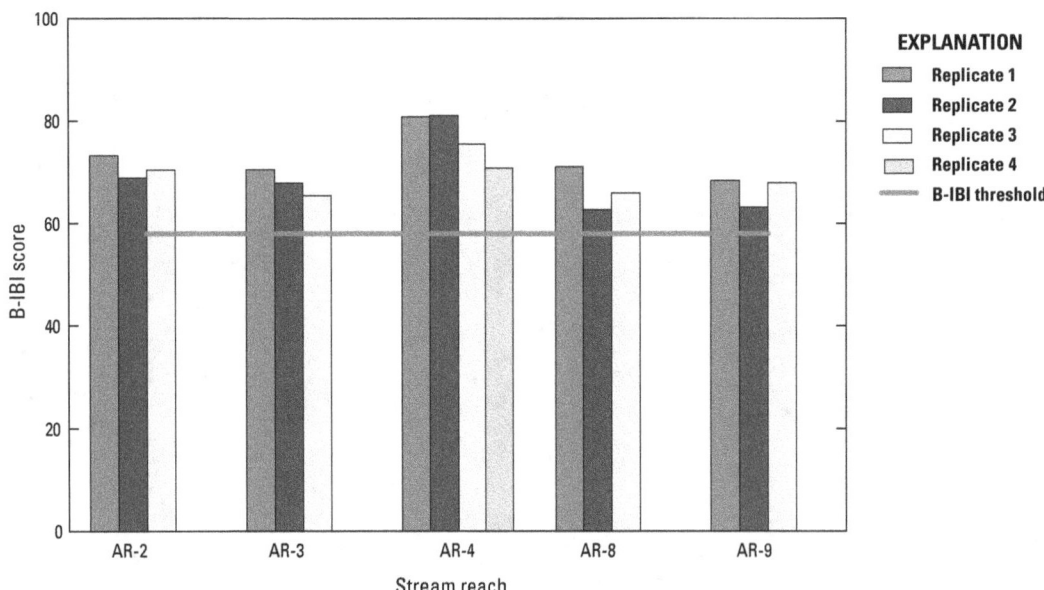

Figure 20. New Hampshire Department of Environmental Services (NHDES) benthic index of biotic integrity (B–IBI) for the Androscoggin River, Coos County, New Hampshire. The reference reach (AR2) is 16 kilometers (km) upstream from a former chloralkali facility in Berlin, N.H., and stream reaches AR3, AR4, AR8, and AR9 are 0 to 16 km downstream from the former chloralkali facility. Three replicate samples were collected at AR2, AR3, AR8, and AR9, and four replicate samples at AR4. The NHDES B–IBI threshold is 58. Stream reaches that score higher than the B–IBI threshold are categorized as unimpaired.

at AR3 compared with other sites was mainly due to greater abundance of Diptera Simuliidae *Simulium,* which presumably favored the steady low-flow water conditions at this site. Abundance downstream from the point source was not significantly different from the reference site (table 4, in back of report). Total taxa (the total number of taxa in the sample) and EPT taxa (taxa in the generally more environmentally sensitive orders Ephemeroptera (mayflies), Plecoptera, and Trichoptera (caddisflies)) were both highest at AR9 (table 5, in back of report); however, there was no significant difference in either metric among the spatial grouping of far (AR8, AR9), near (AR3, AR4), or reference (AR2) stream reaches.

Surface-water THg and MeHg concentrations in the Androscoggin River were all below the Canadian guideline for the protection of aquatic life (table 9; Canadian Council of Ministers of the Environment, 1999). One surface-water THg concentration exceeded the 30-day standard of 1.3 ng/L set by the USEPA for Great Lakes fish-eating wildlife (U.S. Environmental Protection Agency, 1995). Sediment THg concentrations did not exceed the 1,060 ng/g dry weight consensus-based probable effect concentration (PEC) for adverse effects to benthic organisms in any sample (MacDonald and others, 2000), but one-quarter of the sediment samples did exceed the 180 ng/g dry weight consensus-based threshold effects concentration (TEC) for adverse effects to benthic organisms (MacDonald and others, 2000) and the 170 ng/g Canadian interim sediment quality guidelines (ISQG) for the protection of aquatic life (Canadian Council of Ministers of the Environment, 1999). The Wheeler Bay reference site was the only site that had no sediment sample with concentrations above the TEC and ISQG guidelines, and only AR5 had a median sediment THg concentration higher than the TEC and ISQG guidelines. Whereas water and sediment THg were mostly below guidelines, smallmouth bass THg concentrations in all samples (table 9) were higher than guidelines set for fish-eating birds (13 ng/g, kingfisher; Sample and others, 1996), fish-eating mammals (79 ng/g, river otter; Sample and others, 1996), and human health (140 ng/g; U.S. Environmental Protection Agency, 2001c, 2009).

Comparison to Other Studies

Data from the Androscoggin River were compared with datasets from the Northeastern Ecosystems Research Cooperative (NERC) and the USGS NAWQA (Kamman and others, 2005a, b; Shanley and others, 2005; Bauch and others, 2009). The NERC dataset is a compilation of regional stream data from New England, New York, Quebec, Ontario, and the Atlantic provinces of Canada, whereas the NAWQA dataset includes stream data from across the United States. Grouped medians from the Androscoggin River, the NERC, and the NAWQA datasets were compared using a KWRS test. For purposes of comparison, Androscoggin River smallmouth bass THg data from the NERC dataset were combined with data from the study of this report. Androscoggin River sediment THg concentrations were not significantly different than concentrations in the regional or national surveys. Sediment from the Androscoggin River had significantly lower MeHg concentrations than other streams in the Northeastern region but similar MeHg concentrations to streams across the country (table 10). However, comparisons between the surficial sediment from the Androscoggin River study and from other studies may have some bias because the sediment in the Androscoggin River study was sampled to 10 cm, whereas sediments in the NERC and NAWQA studies were generally sampled to 2 cm and never deeper than 5 cm. The greater sampling depth of the Androscoggin sediments could have a diluting effect, lowering THg and MeHg concentrations relative to the other surveys. Smallmouth bass THg concentrations from the Androscoggin River downstream from the point source were significantly higher than smallmouth bass from across the country, but only smallmouth bass from the furthest downstream stream reaches (AR7–AR9) were significantly higher than smallmouth bass from the Northeastern region studies (table 10). Surface-water THg and MeHg concentrations from the Androscoggin River study were similar to those from regional and national studies that focused on uncontaminated or nonpoint source lotic systems; however, the number of observations was too small (n=1–2) for statistical evaluation.

Table 9. Guidelines for total mercury in surface water, sediment, and fish and methylmercury in surface water.

[Guidelines are listed with the percentage of samples from the Androscoggin River that exceeded the guideline shown in brackets. Methylmercury (MeHg) guidelines are used for fish-eating wildlife and human health because more than 95 percent of mercury in smallmouth bass is MeHg. ng/L, nanograms per liter; dw, dry weight; THg, total mercury; ng/g, nanograms per gram; ww, wet weight; --, no data]

Guideline	Unfiltered surface water, in ng/L		THg surfical sediment, in ng/g dw	THg smallmouth bass fillet, in ng/g ww
	THg	MeHg		
Fish-eating wildlife[1]	1.3 [20]	--	--	--
Aquatic life[2]	26 [0]	4 [0]	170 [25]	--
Threshold effects level[3]	--	--	180 [23]	--
Probable effects level[3]	--	--	1,060 [0]	--
Fish-eating mammal[4]	--	--	--	79 [100]
Human health[5]	--	--	--	140 [100]

[1]U.S. Environmental Protection Agency, 1995a.

[2]Canadian Council of Ministers of the Environment, 1999.

[3]MacDonald and others, 2000.

[4]Sample and others, 1996.

[5]U.S. Environmental Protection Agency, 2001c, 2009.

Table 10. Comparison of mercury concentrations in the Androscoggin River, Coos County, New Hampshire, with National Water-Quality Assessment Program and Northeastern Ecosystem Research Cooperative datasets.

[Mercury concentrations are median values; values in bold are statistically different. Letters A, B, and C, indicate which medians are different: A medians are statistically different than B medians, AB medians are not statistically different than A or B but are different from C, and ABC indicates medians are not statistically different than A, B, or C. The nonparametric Kruskal-Wallis rank sum test was run only for sites with at least five samples. Data are from streams only. Numbers in brackets are the number of samples from each site. Data for the Northeastern Ecosystem Research Cooperative (NERC) study were collected from 1983 through 2002; data for the National Water-Quality Assessment Program study were collected from 1998 through 2005; data for the Androscoggin River study were collected from 2009 through 2011. Surficial sediments are from the top 10 centimeters (cm) in the Androscoggin study and the top 2 or 5 cm in other studies. For purposes of comparison, all smallmouth bass lengths were restricted to 25 to 38 cm, and data for smallmouth bass from the NERC dataset have been combined with the Androscoggin River study data. All smallmouth bass samples are fillets. THg, total mercury; MeHg, methylmercury; dw, dry weight; ng/g, nanograms per gram; ng/L, nanograms per liter; ww, wet weight]

Site location	THg unfiltered surface water, in ng/L		MeHg unfiltered surface water, in ng/L		THg surfical sediment, in ng/g dw		MeHg surfical sediment, in ng/g dw		THg smallmouth bass fillet, in ng/g ww	
Androscoggin River data										
Upstream of point source	1.00 [1]		0.05 [1]		30 [11]	AB	0.23 [5]	B	418 [10]	ABC
Downstream near point source	1.02 [2]		0.05 [2]		117 [25]	AB	0.74 [7]	B	528 [26]	AB
Downstream far from point source	1.30 [2]		.06 [2]		111 [35]	AB	0.98 [14]	B	599 [28]	A
Other datasets										
Northeastern North America[1,2,3]	2.20 [388]	A	0.20 [101]	A	160 [182]	A	2.70 [69]	A	410 [179]	B
United States[4]	2.06 [287]	B	0.09 [288]	B	25.4 [296]	B	0.40 [295]	B	273 [46]	C

[1]Shanley and others, 2005.

[2]Kamman and others, 2005b.

[3]Kamman and others, 2005a.

[4]Bauch and others, 2009.

Summary and Conclusions

During operation of the chloralkali facility in Berlin, New Hampshire, elemental mercury (Hg^0) was spilled into the Androscoggin River, contaminating the overburden and underlying fractured rock on the east (left) bank of the Androscoggin River. In September 2005, Congress added the former chloralkali facility in Berlin to the national priorities list, commonly known as the Superfund list. Mercury contamination from historical paper and saw mill activities represents a significant potential risk to human health and the environment.

Total mercury (THg) and methylmercury (MeHg) concentrations in Androscoggin River sediment, pore water, and biota were elevated downstream from the former chloralkali facility relative to reference sites. Sequential extraction of surface sediment showed a distinct difference in mercury speciation upstream compared with downstream from the former chloralkali facility. The reference site was dominated by potassium hydroxide-extractable THg consistent with organic mercury or particle-bound divalent mercury (Hg(II)), whereas sites downstream from the point source were dominated by concentrated nitric acid-extractable THg, indicative of Hg^0 or mercurous chloride. Mercury metrics from the study indicated Hg(II) at the reference site was more available for Hg(II)-methylation compared with sites downstream from the point source, but the absolute concentrations of whole sediment Hg(II)$_R$ and THg in biota were greater downstream from the point source. In addition, whole sediment Hg(II)$_R$ and small-mouth bass THg concentrations appeared to increase further downstream from the point source. The furthest downstream reach (AR9 from Gorham Dam to Shelburne Dam) had larger mass of fine sediment and larger estimated mass inventory of mercury species than any other stream reach by an order of magnitude for both masses.

Sediment organic carbon and bulk density were the dominant influences on sediment THg distribution. The availability of Hg(II) for methylation was best described as a positive function of sediment THg, percent fines, and sediment oxidation reduction potential (redox; E_h). The microbial activity associated with Hg(II)-methylation (as measured by the mercury methylation potential (MPP) constant (k_{meth})) was best described by E_h alone. MPP was primarily a function of sediment THg concentration and E_h.

Toxicity tests and invertebrate community assessment suggest that impairment of invertebrates is not occurring at the current (2009 and 2010) levels of mercury contamination downstream from the point source. Concentrations of THg and MeHg in most water and sediment samples from the Androscoggin River were below Federal and consensus-based guidelines, whereas smallmouth bass mercury concentrations were above U.S. Environmental Protection Agency and regional guidelines in all samples. Smallmouth bass THg concentrations from the Androscoggin River downstream from the point source were significantly higher than those reported in a national survey, but only smallmouth bass mercury concentrations from the furthest downstream stream reaches (Cascade Dam to Shelburne Dam) were significantly higher than those in Northeastern region studies.

The apparent greater potential for Hg(II)-methylation and mercury bioaccumulation in the lower gradient stream reaches of the Androscoggin River may reflect changes in the type and size of particles deposited to the benthos and the speciation and availability of mercury for Hg(II)-methylation associated with those particles. These findings suggest that an even greater potential for Hg(II)-methylation and mercury bioaccumulation may exist as the river gradient continues to flatten downstream from Shelburne Dam.

Selected References

Ainsworth, C.C., Cullinan, V.I., Crecelius, E.A., Wagnon, K.B., and Nielwolny, L.A., 2005, Sample holding time reevaluation: U.S. Environmental Protection Agency EPA/600/R–05/124, 329 p., at http://www.epa.gov/esd/cmb/research/bs_033cmb06.pdf.

Amyot, Marc, Morel, F.M.M., and Ariya, P.A., 2005, Dark oxidation of dissolved and liquid elemental mercury in aquatic environments: Environmental Science and Technology, v. 39, no. 1, p. 110–114.

Avatar Environmental, 2009, Standard operating procedure for fish collection and processing, appendix A *of* Androscoggin River investigation, chloralkali superfund site, Berlin, N.H.: Avatar Environmental [variously paged].

Bauch, N.J., Chasar, L.C., Scudder, B.C., Moran, P.W., Hitt, K.J., Brigham, M.E., Lutz, M.A., and Wentz, D.A., 2009, Data on mercury in water, bed sediment, and fish from streams across the United States, 1998–2005: U.S. Geological Survey Data Series 307, 33 p., accessed January 8, 2013, at http://pubs.usgs.gov/ds/307/.

Blocksom, Karen, 2004, Development of the New Hampshire Benthic Index of Biotic Integrity, *in* Neils, David, 2007, NH benthic index of biotic integrity (B–IBI) for wadeable streams—2006 threshold modification to account for natural variation: New Hampshire Department of Environmental Services, 39 p., accessed January 8, 2013, at http://des nh.gov/organization/divisions/water/wmb/swqa/2006/documents/appendix33.pdf.

Bloom, N.S., Gill, G.A., Cappellino, Steven, Dobbs, Charles, McShea, Larry, Driscoll, Charles, Mason, Robert, and Rudd, John, 1999, Speciation and cycling of mercury in Lavaca Bay, Texas, sediments: Environmental Science and Technology, v. 33, no. 1, p. 7–13.

Bloom, N.S., Preus, Eve, Katon, Jodie, and Hiltner, Misti, 2003, Selective extractions to assess the biogeochemically relevant fractionation of inorganic mercury in sediments and soils: Analytica Chimica Acta, v. 479, p. 233–248.

Buck, David, and Evers, David, 2011, Standard operating procedure for bird and mammal tissue for contaminant analysis, former chloralkali facility, Berlin, N.H., RFP 80013–040 *of* Nobis Engineering, quality assurance project plan, ecological investigation, chloralkali facility (former) superfund site, Berlin, New Hampshire: U.S. Environmental Protection Agency Task Order 0013–RI–CO–01BQ, Remedial Action Contract EP–S1–06–03 [variously paged].

Canadian Council of Ministers of the Environment, 1999, Canadian environmental quality guidelines: Canadian Council of Ministers of the Environment, accessed April 16, 2013, at http://st-ts.ccme.ca/.

Degnan, J.R., Clark, S.F., Harte, P.T., and Mack, T.J., 2005, Geology and preliminary hydrogeological characterization of the Cell-House site, Berlin, New Hampshire, 2003–04: U.S. Geological Survey Scientific Investigations Report 2004–5282, 55 p., 1 pl. (Also available at http://pubs.usgs.gov/sir/2004/5282/.)

Degnan, J.R., Teeple, A.P., Johnston, C.M., Marvin-DiPasquale, M.C., and Luce, Darryl, 2011, Geophysical bed sediment characterization of the Androscoggin River from the former chloralkali facility superfund site, Berlin, New Hampshire, to the state border with Maine, August 2009: U.S. Geological Survey Scientific Investigations Report 2011–5158, 27 p. (Also available at http://pubs.usgs.gov/sir/2011/5158/.)

Dennis, I.F., Clair, T.A., Driscoll, C.T., Kamman, Neil, Chalmers, Ann, Shanley, Jamie, Norton, S.A., and Kahl, Steve, 2005, Distribution patterns of mercury in lakes and rivers of northeastern North America: Ecotoxicology, v. 14, p. 113–123.

Dong, Wenming, Liang, Liyuan, Brooks, Scott, Southworth, George, and Gu, Baohua, 2010, Roles of dissolved organic matter in the speciation of mercury and methylmercury in a contaminated ecosystem in Oak Ridge, Tennessee: Environmental Chemistry, v. 7, no. 1, p. 94.

Environmental Services Assistance Team, 2009a, Two species, 96-hour, acute toxicity testing results using pore water samples collected from the Androscoggin River in areas associated with former chloralkali facility in Berlin, N.H.: U.S. Environmental Protection Agency Task Order 26–04, TDF No. 1501, Project Numbers 09090027 and 09090039, 57 p.

Environmental Services Assistance Team, 2009b, Two species, chronic toxicity testing results using surface water samples collected from the Androscoggin River in areas associated with former chloralkali facility in Berlin, N.H.: U.S. Environmental Protection Agency Task Order 26–04, TDF No. 1501, Project Number 09090023, 46 p.

EnviroSystems, 2010a, 20-day *Hyalella azteca* survival and growth sediment toxicity test, *in* Nobis Engineering, Inc. Project 80013 DAS–RAC2–030, Toxicity evaluation of freshwater sediment samples: U.S. Environmental Protection Agency Task Order 10–NH–80013–045–TO–01, p. 14.

EnviroSystems, 2010b, 20-day *Chironomus dilutes* survival and growth sediment toxicity test, *in* Nobis Engineering, Inc. Project 80013 DAS–RAC2–030, Toxicity evaluation of freshwater sediment samples: U.S. Environmental Protection Agency Task Order 10–NH–80013–045–TO–01, p. 13.

Gerbig, C.A., Kim, C.S., Stegemeier, J.P., Ryan, J.N., and Aiken, G.R., 2011, Formation of nanocolloidal metacinnabar in mercury-DOM-sulfide systems: Environmental Science and Technology, v. 45, no. 21, p. 9180–9187.

Gilmour, C.C., Henry, E.A., and Mitchell, R., 1992, Sulfate stimulation of mercury methylation in freshwater sediments: Environmental Science and Technology, v. 26, p. 2281–2287.

Hammerschmidt, C.R., and Fitzgerald, W.F., 2006, Methyl-mercury cycling in sediments on the continental shelf of southern New England: Geochimica et Cosmochimica Acta, v. 70, no. 4, p. 918–930.

Han, S., Obraztsova, A., Pretto, P., Choe, K.Y., Gieskes, J., Deheyn, D.D., and Tebo, B.M., 2007, Biogeochemical factors affecting mercury methylation in sediments of the Venice Lagoon, Italy: Environmental Toxicology and Chemistry, v. 26, no. 4, p. 655–663.

Helsel, D.R., 2005, Nondetects and data analysis—Statistics for censored environmental data: New York, John Wiley & Sons, Inc., 250 p.

Hill, J.R., O'Driscoll, N.J., and Lean, D.R.S., 2009, Size distribution of methylmercury associated with particulate and dissolved organic matter in freshwaters: Science of the Total Environment, v. 408, no. 2, p. 408–414.

Horvat, Milena, Liang, Lian, and Bloom, N.S., 1993, Comparison of distillation with other current isolation methods for the determination of methyl mercury compounds in low level environment samples—Part II. Water: Analytica Chimica Acta, v. 282, p. 153–168.

Huerta-Diaz, M.A., and Morse, J.W., 1992, Pyritization of trace metals in anoxic marine sediments: Geochimica et Cosmochimica Acta, v. 56, p. 2681–2702.

Kamman, N.C., Burgess, N.M., Driscoll, C.T., Simonin, H.A., Goodale, Wing, Linehan, Janice, Estabrook, Robert, Hutcheson, Michael, Major, Andrew, Scheuhammer, A.M., and Scruton, D.A., 2005a, Mercury in freshwater fish of northeast North America—A geographic perspective based on fish tissue monitoring databases: Ecotoxicology, v. 14, nos. 1–2, p. 163–180.

Kamman, N.C., Chalmers, Ann, Clair, T.A., Major, Andrew, Moore, R.B., Norton, S.A., and Shanley, J.B., 2005b, Factors influencing mercury in freshwater surface sediments of northeast North America: Ecotoxicology, v. 14, nos. 1–2, p. 101–111.

Kendall, Carol, Silva, S.R., and Kelly, V.J., 2001, Carbon and nitrogen isotopic compositions of particulate organic matter in four large river systems across the United States: Hydrological Processes, v. 15, no. 7, p. 1301–1346.

Krabbenhoft, D.P., Wiener, J.G., Brumbaugh, W.G., Olson, M.L., DeWild, J.F., and Sabin, T.J., 1999, A national pilot study of mercury contamination of aquatic ecosystems along multiple gradients: U.S. Geological Survey Water-Resources Investigations Report 99–4018B [not paged]. (Also available at http://toxics.usgs.gov/pubs/wri99-4018/Volume2/sectionB/2301_Krabbenhoft/index.html.)

Lambertsson, Lars, and Nilsson, Mats, 2006, Organic material—The primary control on mercury methylation and ambient methyl mercury concentrations in estuarine sediments: Environmental Science and Technology, v. 40, no. 6, p. 1822–1829.

Lutz, M.A., Brigham, M.E., and Marvin-DiPasquale, Mark, 2008, Procedures for collecting and processing streambed sediment and pore water for analysis of mercury as part of the National Water-Quality Assessment Program: U.S. Geological Survey Open-File Report 2008–1279, 68 p. (Also available at http://pubs.usgs.gov/of/2008/1279/.)

MacDonald, D.D., Ingersoll, C.G., and Berger, T.A., 2000, Development and evaluation of consensus-based sediment quality guidelines for freshwater ecosystems: Archives of Environmental Contamination and Toxicology, v. 39, no. 1, p. 20–31.

Maine Department of Environmental Protection, 2009, Surface Water Ambient Toxics Monitoring Program—2009 final report: Augusta, Maine, Maine Department of Environmental Protection, 168 p., accessed January 14, 2013, at http://www.maine.gov/dep/water/monitoring/toxics/swat/2009/2009_SWAT_report_final.pdf.

Marvin-DiPasquale, M.C., and Agee, J.L., 2003, Microbial mercury cycling in sediments of the San Francisco Bay-Delta: Estuaries, v. 26, p. 1517–1528.

Marvin-DiPasquale, M.C., Agee, J.L., Kakouros, Evangelos, Kieu, L.H., Fleck, J.A., and Alpers, C.N., 2011, The effects of sediment and mercury mobilization in the South Yuba River and Humbug Creek confluence area, Nevada County, California—Concentrations, speciation and environmental fate—Part 2. Laboratory experiments: U.S. Geological Survey Open-File Report 2010–1325B, 53 p., accessed January 14, 2013, at http://pubs.usgs.gov/of/2010/1325B.

Marvin-DiPasquale, M.C., Alpers, C.N., and Fleck, J.A., 2009b, Mercury, methylmercury, and other constituents in sediment and water from seasonal and permanent wetlands in the Cache Creek Settling basin and Yolo bypass, Yolo County, California, 2005–06: U.S. Geological Survey Open-File Report 2009–1182, 69 p., accessed January 14, 2013, at http://pubs.usgs.gov/of/2009/1182/.

Marvin-DiPasquale, M.C., and Cox, M.H., 2007, Legacy mercury in Alviso Slough, south San Francisco Bay, California—Concentration, speciation and mobility: U.S. Geological Survey Open-File Report 2007–1240, 98 p. (Also available at http://pubs.usgs.gov/of/2007/1240/.)

Marvin-DiPasquale, M.C., Hall, B.D., Flanders, J.R., Ladizinski, N., Agee, J.L., Kieu, L.H., and Windham-Myer, Lisamarie, 2006, Ecosystem investigations of benthic methylmercury production—A tin-reduction approach for assessing the inorganic mercury pool available for methylation: Mercury 2006—Eighth International Conference on Mercury as a Global Pollutant, Madison, Wisc., August 6–11, 2006 [abstract].

Marvin-DiPasquale, M.C., Lutz, M.A., Brigham, M.E., Krabbenhoft, D.P., Aiken, G.R., Orem, W.H., and Hall, B.D., 2009a, Mercury cycling in stream ecosystems—2. Benthic methylmercury production and bed sediment-pore water partitioning: Environmental Science and Technology, v. 43, no. 8, p. 2726–2732.

Marvin-DiPasquale, M.C., Lutz, M.A., Krabbenhoft, D.P., Aiken, G.R., Orem, W.H., Hall, B.D., DeWild, J.F., and Brigham, M.E., 2008, Total mercury, methylmercury, methylmercury production potential, and ancillary streambed-sediment and pore water data for selected streams in Oregon, Wisconsin, and Florida, 2003–04: U.S. Geological Survey Data Series 375, 25 p. (Also available at http://pubs.usgs.gov/ds/375/.)

Matthes, W.J., Jr., Sholar, C.J., and George, J.R., 1992, Quality-assurance plan for the analysis of fluvial sediment by laboratories of the U.S. Geological Survey: U.S. Geological Survey Open-File Report 91–467, 37 p. (Also available at http://pubs.usgs.gov/of/1991/0467/report.pdf.)

Morel, F.M.M., Kraepiel, A.M.L., and Amyot, Marc, 1998, The chemical cycle and bioaccumulation of mercury: Annual Review of Ecology and Systematics, v. 29, p. 543–566.

Neils, David, 2007, NH benthic index of biotic integrity (B–IBI) for wadeable streams—2006 threshold modification to account for natural variation: New Hampshire Department of Environmental Services, 39 p., accessed January 8, 2013, at http://des.nh.gov/organization/divisions/water/wmb/swqa/2006/documents/appendix33.pdf.

New Hampshire Department of Environmental Services, 2004, Biomonitoring program protocols: New Hampshire Department of Environmental Services, accessed January 8, 2013, at http://des.nh.gov/organization/divisions/water/wmb/biomonitoring/documents/protocols.pdf.

Nobis Engineering, 2009, Appendix B—Fish sampling plan and biological sampling plan, *in* Quality assurance project plan, ecological investigation, chloralkali facility (former) superfund site, Berlin, New Hampshire: U.S. Environmental Protection Agency Task Order 0013–RI–CO–01BQ, Remedial Action Contract EP–S1–06–03 [variously paged].

Nobis Engineering, 2011, Appendix A—Ecological investigation QAPP sampling SOP reference S–3, Standard operating procedure tree swallow sampling and tissue processing, *in* Quality assurance project plan, ecological investigation, chloralkali facility (former) superfund site, Berlin, New Hampshire: U.S. Environmental Protection Agency Task Order 0013–RI–CO–01BQ, Remedial Action Contract EP–S1–06–03 [variously paged].

Olson, M.L., and DeWild, J.F., 1999, Techniques for the collection and species-specific analysis of low levels of mercury in water, sediment, and biota, *in* U.S. Geological Survey Toxic Substances Hydrology Program—Proceedings of the technical meeting, Charleston, South Carolina, March 8–12, 1999: U.S. Geological Survey Water-Resources Investigations Report 99–4018B, p. 191–200. (Also available at http://toxics.usgs.gov/pubs/wri99-4018/Volume2/sectionB/2305_Olson/.)

Olund, S.D., DeWild, J.F., Olson, M.L., and Tate, M.T., 2004, Methods for the preparation and analysis of solids and suspended solids for total mercury: U.S. Geological Survey Techniques and Methods, book 5, chap. A8, 23 p. (Also available at http://pubs.usgs.gov/tm/2005/tm5A8/.)

Parker, J.L., and Bloom, N.S., 2005, Preservation and storage techniques for low-level aqueous mercury speciation: Science of the Total Environment, v. 337, nos. 1–3, p. 253–263.

Sample, B.E., Opresko, D.M., and Suter, G.W., 1996, Toxicological benchmarks for wildlife, 1996: Oak Ridge, Tenn., Oak Ridge National Laboratory, Publication ES/ER/TM–86/R3, 43 p.

Scudder, B.C., Chasar, L.C., Wentz, D.A., Bauch, N.J., Brigham, M.E., Moran, P.W., and Krabbenhoft, D.P., 2009, Mercury in fish, bed sediment, water from streams across the United States, 1998–2005: U.S. Geological Survey Scientific Investigations Report 2009–5109, 74 p. (Also available at http://pubs.usgs.gov/sir/2009/5109/.)

Shanley, J.B., Kamman, N.C., Clair, T.A., and Chalmers, A.T., 2005, Physical controls on total and methylmercury concentrations in streams and lakes of northeastern USA: Ecotoxicology, v. 14, p. 125–134.

Shelton, L.R., and Capel, P.D., 1994, Guidelines for collecting and processing samples of stream bed sediment for analysis of trace elements and organic contaminants for the National Water-Quality Assessment Program: U.S. Geological Survey Open-File Report 94–458, 20 p. (Also available at http://water.usgs.gov/nawqa/pnsp/pubs/ofr94-458/.)

Slowey, A.J., 2010, Rate of formation and dissolution of mercury sulfide nanoparticles—The dual role of natural organic matter: Geochimica et Cosmochimica Acta, v. 74, p. 4693–4708.

Sunderland, E.M., Gobas, F.A.P.C., Branfireun, B.A., and Heyes, Andrew, 2006, Environmental controls on the speciation and distribution of mercury in coastal sediments: Marine Chemistry, v. 102, p. 111–123.

U.S. Environmental Protection Agency, 1995, Great Lakes water quality initiative technical support document for wildlife criteria: U.S. Environmental Protection Agency 820–B95–009, 53 p.

U.S. Environmental Protection Agency, 2000, Methods for measuring the toxicity and bioaccumulation of sediment-associated contaminants with freshwater invertebrates (2d ed.): U.S. Environmental Protection Agency EPA/600–R–99/064, 192 p.

U.S. Environmental Protection Agency, 2001a, Acute (96-hour) reference toxicity test methods for *Hyalella azteca* and *Chironomous tentans*: U.S. Environmental Protection Agency, Biology Section, Standard Operating Procedure [variously paged].

U.S. Environmental Protection Agency, 2001b, Appendix to method 1631—Total mercury in tissue, sludge, sediment, and soil by acid digestion and BrCl oxidation: U.S. Environmental Protection Agency EPA–821–R–01–013, 13 p. (Also available at http://www.tekran.com/files/EPA_1631_Appendix_for_Solids.pdf.)

U.S. Environmental Protection Agency, 2001c, Water quality criterion for protection of human health—Methylmercury: U.S. Environmental Protection Agency Technical Report EPA/823/R–01/001 [variously paged].

U.S. Environmental Protection Agency, 2002, Method 1631, revision E—Mercury in water by oxidation, purge and trap, and cold vapor atomic fluorescence spectrometry: U.S. Environmental Protection Agency EPA–821–R–02–019, 38 p. (Also available at http://water.epa.gov/scitech/methods/cwa/metals/mercury/index.cfm.)

U.S. Environmental Protection Agency, 2005, National priorities list for uncontrolled hazardous waste sites: Federal Register, v. 70, no. 177, September 14, 2005, p. 54286–54293, accessed January 10, 2013, at http://www.gpo.gov/fdsys/pkg/FR-2005-09-14/pdf/05-18235.pdf.

U.S. Environmental Protection Agency, 2008a, Chronic toxicity method for *Ceriodaphnia dubia* (revision 5.0): U.S. Environmental Protection Agency, Biology Section Standard Operating Procedure, Office of Environmental Measurements and Evaluation, U.S. Environmental Protection Agency, Region 1.

U.S. Environmental Protection Agency, 2008b, Chronic toxicity method for *Pimephales promelas* (revision 6.0): U.S. Environmental Protection Agency, Biology Section Standard Operating Procedure, Office of Environmental Measurements and Evaluation, U.S. Environmental Protection Agency, Region 1.

U.S. Environmental Protection Agency, 2010, Guidance for implementing the January 2001 methylmercury water quality criterion: Washington D.C., Office of Water, EPA–823–R–10–001, 209 p., accessed February 4, 2013, at http://water.epa.gov/scitech/swguidance/standards/criteria/aqlife/methylmercury/upload/mercury2010.pdf.

U.S. Geological Survey, 2005, National field manual for the collection of water-quality data: U.S. Geological Survey Techniques of Water-Resources Investigations, book 9, 46 p.

Weston Solutions, Inc., 2005, Site Investigation Report—Former Chlor Alkali Facility below Saw Mill Dam: Berlin, N.H., February 10, 2004, 203 p.

Wilde, F.D., 2008, Field measurements: U.S. Geological Survey Techniques of Water-Resources Investigations, book 9, chap. A6, accessed January 15, 2013, at http://pubs.water.usgs.gov/twri9A6/.

Xianchao, Y., Chandrasekhar, T.M., and Tate, K., 2005, Analysis of methylmercury in sediment and tissue by KOH/CH3OH digestion followed by aqueous phase ethylation: Florida Department of Environmental Protection HG–003–2.2.

Yeardley, R.B., Jr., Lazorchak, J.M., and Paulsen, S.G., 1998, Elemental fish tissue contamination in northeastern U.S. lakes—Evaluation of an approach to regional assessment: Environmental Toxicology and Chemistry, v. 17, no. 9, p. 1875–1884.

Zimmerman, M.J., Massey, A.J., and Campo, K.W., 2005, Pushpoint sampling for defining spatial and temporal variations in contaminant concentrations in sediment pore water near the ground-water/surface water interface: U.S. Geological Survey Scientific Investigations Report 2005–5036, 70 p. (Also available at http://pubs.usgs.gov/sir/2005/5036/.)

Tables 2, 4, 5, and 6

Table 2.   Summary of methods used for analysis of sediment, pore water, surface water, and biota from the Androscoggin River, Coos County, New Hampshire

[USGS, U.S. Geological Survey; NRP, National Research Program; USEPA, U.S. Environmental Protection Agency; NERL, New England Regional Laboratory]

Notation	Type of data	Collection period	Source of data	Method and (or) method citation
Sediment mercury parameters				
THg	Total mercury	2009	Als Laboratory Group, Salt Lake City, Utah	ILM05.4, USEPA (2006).
		2010	USGS NRP Laboratory, Menlo Park, Calif.	Marvin-DiPasquale and others (2011).
MeHg	Methylmercury	2009	Columbia Analytical Services, Kelso, Wash.	1630, USEPA (1998).
		2010	USGS NRP Laboratory	Marvin-DiPasquale and others (2011).
$Hg(II)_R$	Inorganic reactive mercury	2010	USGS NRP Laboratory	Marvin-DiPasquale and others (2011).
$Hg(II)_{KOH}$	1M potassium hydroxide (KOH)-extractable mercury	2009	Columbia Analytical Services	Bloom and others (2003).
THg, F1 thru F5	Sequential extraction	2010	USGS NRP Laboratory	Bloom and others (2003).
k_{meth}	MeHg production potential rate constant	2010	USGS NRP Laboratory	Marvin-DiPasquale and others (2011).
MPP	MeHg production potential rate (calculated)	2010	USGS NRP Laboratory	Marvin-DiPasquale and others (2011).
Sediment nonmercury parameters				
TAL metals	Target analyte list metals	2009	Als Laboratory Group	ILM05.4, USEPA (2006).
SEM metals	Simultaneously extractable metals	2009	Columbia Analytical Services	SW6010, USEPA (1991).
AVS	Acid volatile sulfur	2009	Columbia Analytical Services	Draft 1991, USEPA (1991).
Dioxin/furans	Dioxin and furans	2009	SGS Environmental, Wilmington, N.C.	SW8290, USEPA (2005).
PCB	Polychlorinated biphenyl	2009	SGS Environmental	CBC0.10, USEPA (2007).
Pesticides	Pesticides	2009	Columbia Analytical Services	SW8081, USEPA (2007).
SVOCs	Semivolital organic compounds	2009	Columbia Analytical Services	SW8270, USEPA (2007).
H. azteca toxicity	*Hyalella azteca* survival and biomass	2009, 2010	EnviroSystems, Inc., Hampton, N.H.	100.4 and 100.5, USEPA (2000).
C. dilutus toxicity	*Chironomus dilutus* survival and biomass	2009, 2010	EnviroSystems, Inc.	100.4 and 100.5, USEPA (2000).
TRS	Total reduced sulfur	2010	USGS NRP Laboratory	Marvin-DiPasquale and others (2008).
$Fe(II)_{AE}$	Acid extractable ferrous iron (Fe(II))	2010	USGS NRP Laboratory	Marvin-DiPasquale and others (2008).
$Fe(III)_a$	Amorphous (poorly crystalline) ferric iron (Fe(III))	2010	USGS NRP Laboratory	Marvin-DiPasquale and others (2008).
$Fe(III)_c$	Crystalline ferric iron (Fe(III))	2010	USGS NRP Laboratory	Marvin-DiPasquale and others (2008).
%LOI	Percentage of weight loss on ignition	2010	USGS NRP Laboratory	Marvin-DiPasquale and others (2008).
TC	Total carbon	2010	USGS NRP Laboratory	Kendall and others (2001).
TN	Total nitrogen	2010	USGS NRP Laboratory	Kendall and others (2001).
TOC	Total organic carbon	2009	Columbia Analytical Services	SW9060, USEPA (2007).
		2010	USGS NRP Laboratory	Kendall and others (2001).
$\delta^{13}C$	Carbon 13 (^{13}C) isotope	2010	USGS NRP Laboratory	Kendall and others (2001).
$\delta^{15}N$	Nitrogen 15 (^{15}N) isotope	2010	USGS NRP Laboratory	Kendall and others (2001).

Table 2   43

Table 2. Summary of methods used for analysis of sediment, pore water, surface water, and biota from the Androscoggin River, Coos County, New Hampshire.—Continued

[USGS, U.S. Geological Survey; NRP, National Research Program; USEPA, U.S. Environmental Protection Agency; NERL, New England Regional Laboratory]

Notation	Type of data	Collection period	Source of data	Method and (or) method citation
			Sediment nonmercury parameters—Continued	
BD	Bulk density	2010	USGS NRP Laboratory	Marvin-DiPasquale and others (2008).
%dry wt	Percent dry weight	2009	Columbia Analytical Services	APHA-AWWA-WPCF (1992).
		2010	USGS NRP Laboratory	Marvin-DiPasquale and others (2008).
%fines	Percent grain size (<74 micrometers (µm))	2009	Columbia Analytical Services	ASTM D422, Plumb (1981), USEPA (1996).
	Percent grain size (<63 µm)	2010	USGS NRP Laboratory	Matthes and others (1992).
E_h	Oxidation-reduction potential	2010	USGS NRP Laboratory	Marvin-DiPasquale and others (2008).
pH	pH	2010	USGS NRP Laboratory	Marvin-DiPasquale and others (2008).
			Pore-water mercury parameters	
pw.THg	Total mercury	2009	Columbia Analytical Services	E1631, USEPA (2001, 2002).
		2010	USGS NRP Laboratory	Marvin-DiPasquale and others (2011).
pw.MeHg	Methylmercury	2009	Columbia Analytical Services	1630, USEPA (1998).
		2010	USGS NRP Laboratory	Marvin-DiPasquale and others (2011).
pw.Hg(II)$_{KOH}$	1M KOH extractable mercury	2009	Columbia Analytical Services	Bloom (2009).
			Pore-water nonmercury parameters	
TAL metals	Target analyte list metals	2009	Als Laboratory Group	ILM05.4, USEPA (2006).
pw.SO$_4$	Sulfate	2009	Columbia Analytical Services	E300.0, USEPA (1982).
		2010	USGS NRP Laboratory	Marvin-DiPasquale and others (2008).
pw.Fe(II)	Ferrous iron	2010	USGS NRP Laboratory	Marvin-DiPasquale and others (2008).
pw.Cl	Chloride	2010	USGS NRP Laboratory	Marvin-DiPasquale and others (2008).
C. tentans toxicity	*Chironomus tentans* survival	2009, 2010	USEPA NERL, Chelmsford, Mass.	Acute 96-hour bioassay, USEPA (2001).
H. azteca toxicity	*Hyalella azteca* survival	2009, 2010	USEPA NERL	Acute 96-hour bioassay, USEPA (2001).
pw.DOC	Dissolved organic carbon	2009	Columbia Analytical Services	SW9060, USEPA (2007).
		2010	USGS NRP Laboratory	
pw.E_h	Oxidation-reduction potential	2009, 2010	USGS field parameter	Wilde (2008).
pw.pH	pH	2009, 2010	USGS field parameter	Wilde (2008).

Table 2. Summary of methods used for analysis of sediment, pore water, surface water, and biota from the Androscoggin River, Coos County, New Hampshire.—Continued

[USGS, U.S. Geological Survey; NRP, National Research Program; USEPA, U.S. Environmental Protection Agency; NERL, New England Regional Laboratory]

Notation	Type of data	Collection period	Source of data	Method and (or) method citation
		Surface-water mercury parameters		
THg	Total mercury	2009	Columbia Analytical Services	E1631, USEPA (2001, 2002).
MeHg	Methylmercury	2009	Columbia Analytical Services	1630, USEPA (1998).
$Hg(II)_{KOH}$	1M KOH-extractable mercury	2009	Columbia Analytical Services	Bloom (2009).
		Surface-water nonmercury parameters		
TAL metals	Target analyte list metals	2009	Als Laboratory Group	ILM05.4, USEPA (2006).
SO_4	Sulfate	2009	Columbia Analytical Services	E300.0, USEPA (1982).
C. dubia toxicity	*Ceriodaphnia dubia* survival & reproduction	2009	USEPA NERL	Chronic 7-day bioassay, USEPA (2008a,b).
P. promelas toxicity	*Pimephales promelas* survival & biomass	2009	USEPA NERL	Chronic 7-day bioassay, USEPA (2008a,b).
TOC	Total organic carbon	2009	Columbia Analytical Services	SW9060, USEPA (2007).
E_h	Oxidation-reduction potential	2010	USGS field parameter	Wilde and others (2005).
pH	pH	2009, 2010	USGS field parameter	Wilde and others (2005).
		Biota mercury parameters		
THg	Total mercury	2009	Columbia Analytical Services	E1631, USEPA (2001, 2002).
		2010, 2011	USEPA NERL	Milestone Inc. Direct Mercury Analyzer operation manual (2008).
		Biota nonmercury parameters		
Invertebrate assemblages		2009	Lotic Inc., Unity, Maine	Neils (2007); New Hampshire Department of Environmental Services (2004).

Table 4   45

Table 4. Wilcoxon rank sum test comparing results upstream and downstream from a former chloralkali site on the Androscoggin River in Berlin, New Hampshire.

[The nonparametric Wilcoxon rank sum (WRS) test comparison of medians grouped either upstream (reference, AR1 and (or) AR2) or downstream from a former chloralkali site (AR3 to AR9). The first quartile (25th percentile (%)), median (50th percentile (%)), and third quartile (75th %) are shown, along with results from all mercury metric comparisons. Only significant results for sediment and pore-water nonmercury metrics are shown. Parameter notations are listed in table 2. dw, dry weight; EPT, Ephemeroptera, Plecoptera, Trichoptera; g/cm³, grams per cubic centimeter; L/kg, liters per kilogram; µm, micrometer; mg, milligrams; mg/g, milligrams per gram; mg/kg, milligrams per kilogram; mL/cm³, milliliters per cubic centimeter; N, (number of observations); ng/g, nanograms per gram; ng/L, nanograms per liter; NS, nonsignificant differences between groupings at a probability level of p less than 0.05; pg/g/d, picograms per gram per day; ww, wet weight; <, less than; †, significant differences between groupings at a probability level of p less than 0.05]

Parameter	Media — Units of measurement	Media — Years	Reference stream reach — 25th %	Reference stream reach — Median	Reference stream reach — 75th %	Reference stream reach — N	Downstream stream reaches — 25th %	Downstream stream reaches — Median	Downstream stream reaches — 75th %	Downstream stream reaches — N	Downstream stream reaches — WRS
Sediment mercury parameters											
THg	ng/g dw	2009, 2010	22	30	69	(11)	89	114	184	-60	†
Hg(II)$_R$	ng/g dw	2010	0.09	0.11	0.13	(8)	0.14	0.18	0.27	-52	†
%Hg(II)$_R$	% of THg	2010	0.37	0.46	0.53	(8)	0.08	0.15	0.23	-52	†
MeHg	ng/g dw	2009, 2010	0.21	0.23	0.47	(5)	0.65	0.96	1.26	-21	†
%MeHg	% of THg	2009, 2010	1.26	1.4	1.54	(2)	0.47	0.6	0.97	-15	NS
k_{meth}	per day	2010	0.0083	0.0087	0.009	(2)	0.0056	0.0095	0.0149	-13	NS
MPP	pg/g/d dw	2010	0.64	0.79	0.95	(2)	1.03	2.11	3.68	-13	NS
K_d[THg]	L/kg	2010	4.47	4.61	4.75	(2)	4.53	4.88	5.07	-13	NS
K_d[MeHg]	L/kg	2010	3.26	3.3	3.33	(2)	3.01	3.24	3.5	-13	NS
Pore-water mercury parameters											
pw.THg	ng/L	2009, 2010	0.26	0.7	1.35	(5)	1.15	1.72	5.93	-20	NS
pw.MeHg	ng/L	2009, 2010	0.06	0.1	0.1	(5)	0.09	0.3	0.59	-20	†
pw.%MeHg	% of THg	2009, 2010	10.83	21.07	29.36	(3)	12.02	23.98	38.44	-15	NS
Biota total mercury											
Oligochaete	ng/g ww	2009	18	20	22	(5)	25	31	40	-19	†
Crayfish	ng/g ww	2009, 2011	50	59	64	(12)	72	89	110	-39	†
WS	ng/g ww	2009, 2011	119	132	135	(7)	136	208	278	-19	†
SMB	ng/g ww	2009, 2011	390	418	421	(10)	511	587	638	-38	†
Bat fur	ng/g ww	2010	4,369	5,062	6,372	(11)	11,920	56,830	118,400	-27	†
Bat blood	ng/g ww	2010	166	233	312	(4)	318	428	566	-12	NS
Swallow feather-adult	ng/g ww	2010	996	1,128	1,324	(14)	997	1,417	1,644	-20	NS
Swallow feather-nestling	ng/g ww	2010	1,059	1,309	1,447	(13)	1,644	1,647	2,118	-9	†
Swallow blood-adult	ng/g ww	2010	288	306	343	(11)	433	520	585	-14	†
Swallow blood-nestling	ng/g ww	2010	30	40	40	(13)	42	53	73	-9	†
Swallow egg	ng/g ww	2010	495	527	568	(13)	607	773	803	-15	†
Sediment sequential extractions											
F1: water	ng/g dw	2010	0.03	0.03	0.04	(2)	0.02	0.05	0.07	-13	NS
	% of THg	2010	0.09	0.1	0.11	(2)	0.01	0.02	0.03	-13	NS

Table 4. Wilcoxon rank sum test comparing results upstream and downstream from a former chloralkali site on the Androscoggin River in Berlin, New Hampshire.—Continued

[The nonparametric Wilcoxon rank sum (WRS) test comparison of medians grouped either upstream (reference, AR1 and (or) AR2) or downstream from a former chloralkali site (AR3 to AR9). The first quartile (25th percentile (%), median (50th %), and third quartile (75th %) are shown, along with results from all mercury metric comparisons. Only significant results for sediment and pore-water nonmercury metrics are shown. Parameter notations are listed in table 2. dw, dry weight; EPT, Ephemeroptera, Plecoptera, Trichoptera; g/cm³, grams per cubic centimeter; L/kg, liters per kilogram; µm, micrometer; mg, milligrams; mg/g, milligrams per gram; mg/kg, milligrams per kilogram; mL/cm³, milliliters per cubic centimeter; N, (number of observations); ng/g, nanograms per gram; ng/L, nanograms per liter; NS, nonsignificant differences between groupings at a probability level of p less than 0.05; pg/g/d, picograms per gram per day; ww, wet weight; <, less than; †, significant differences between groupings at a probability level of p less than 0.05]

Parameter	Media Units of measurement	Years	Reference stream reach				Downstream stream reaches				WRS
			25th %	Median	75th %	N	25th %	Median	75th %	N	
			Sediment sequential extractions—Continued								
F2: 0.1 M acetic acid	ng/g dw	2010	0.02	0.02	0.03	(2)	0.02	0.02	0.03	-13	NS
	% of THg	2010	0.07	0.08	0.09	(2)	0.01	0.02	0.02	-13	†
F3: 1.0 M KOH	ng/g dw	2010	23.4	27.3	31.3	(2)	56.3	70.9	111	-13	†
	% of THg	2010	87.2	87.6	88.1	(2)	38.2	45	58.9	-13	†
F4: 12 M HNO₃	ng/g dw	2010	2.69	2.98	3.26	(2)	43.9	71.3	87.2	-13	†
	% of THg	2010	9.36	9.83	10.3	(2)	39.3	49.9	55.8	-13	†
F5: Aqua Regia	ng/g dw	2010	0.62	0.74	0.86	(2)	3.1	3.9	7.2	-13	†
	% of THg	2010	2.29	2.35	2.4	(2)	2.18	2.65	5.77	-13	NS
			Sediment nonmercury parameters								
Fe(II)$_{AE}$	mg/g dw	2010	3.92	4.39	4.86	(2)	1.66	2.29	3.07	-13	†
AVS	mg/kg dw	2009	17.8	17.8	25.7	(3)	2.07	2.41	3	-8	†
Bulk density	g/cm³ ww	2010	1.32	1.37	1.46	(8)	1.47	1.55	1.67	-52	†
% fines	% <74 µm	2009	55	56.3	60	(3)	25.5	32.2	42.1	-8	†
	% <63 µm	2010	63.1	72.1	75.3	(8)	27.9	44.8	56.4	-52	†
Porosity	mL/cm³ ww	2010	0.64	0.72	0.74	(8)	0.53	0.59	0.64	-52	†
pct.DW	% of ww	2009, 2010	43	46	56	(11)	56	61	68	-60	†
			Sediment toxicity								
Hyalella.azteca.survival	%	2009, 2010	78	80	80	(5)	74	79	85	-21	NS
Hyalella.azteca.biomass	mg dw	2009, 2010	0.38	0.39	0.4	(5)	0.34	0.43	0.5	-21	NS
Chironomus.dilutus.survival	%	2009, 2010	70	76	83	(5)	61	75	80	-21	NS
Chironomus.dilutus.biomass	mg dw	2009, 2010	0.44	0.5	1.25	(5)	0.3	1.15	1.29	-21	NS
			Pore-water toxicity								
Chironomus.tentans.survival	%	2009, 2010	80	90	100	(5)	80	90	100	-21	NS
Hyalella.azteca.survival	%	2009, 2010	70	80	80	(5)	90	100	100	-21	†
			Invertebrate metrics								
Abundance		2009	288	316	486	(3)	148	604	1,020	-12	NS
Total taxa		2009	14	14	15	(3)	9.9	12	13	-12	NS
EPT taxa		2009	16	16	16	(3)	13	15	17	-12	NS

Table 5   47

Table 5. Kruskal-Wallis rank sum test results comparing data grouped by sample distance from a former chloralkali site on the Androscoggin River in Berlin, New Hampshire.

[The nonparametric Kruskal-Wallis rank sum (KWRS) test comparison of medians grouped by distance from a former chloralkali site. The reference reach (AR2) is 16 kilometers (km) upstream from the former chloralkali site; near-stream reaches (AR3–AR6) are 0 to 4 km downstream from the former chloralkali site; far-stream reaches (AR7–AR9) are 8 to 16 km downstream from the former chloralkali site. The first quartile (25th percentile (%)), median (50th %), and third quartile (75th %) are shown, along with results for all mercury metric comparisons. Only significant results for nonmercury metrics are shown. Tukey multiple-comparison test was used to determine rankings on data KWRS indicated as significant. Letters A and B, indicate which medians are different. A medians are statistically different than B medians, and AB medians are not statistically different than A or B. Parameter notation definitions are listed in table 2. dw, dry weight; EPT, Ephemeroptera, Plecoptera, Trichoptera; g/cm³, grams per cubic centimeter; L/kg, liters per kilogram; mg, milligrams; mL/cm³, milliliters per cubic centimeter; μm, micrometers; mv, millivolts; N, (number of observations); ng/g, nanograms per gram; ng/L, nanograms per liter; NS, nonsignificant differences between groupings at a probability level of p less than 0.05; pg/g/d, picograms per gram per day; THg, total mercury; ww, wet weight; <, less than; †, significant differences between groupings at a probability level of p less than 0.05]

Parameter	Media Units of measurement	Year	Reference stream reach				Near stream reaches				Far stream reaches				KWRS
			25th %	Median	75th %	N	25th %	Median	75th %	N	25th %	Median	75th %	N	
Sediment mercury parameters															
THg	ng/g dw	2009, 2010	21	26 B	30	(11)	84	117 A	240	(25)	82	111 AB	160	(35)	†
Hg(II)$_R$	ng/g dw	2010	0.09	0.11 B	0.13	(8)	0.12	0.16 B	0.22	(24)	0.14	0.21 A	0.36	(28)	†
%Hg(II)$_R$	% of THg	2010	0.37	0.46 AB	0.53	(8)	0.07	0.12 B	0.18	(24)	0.13	0.17 A	0.32	(28)	†
MeHg	ng/g dw	2009, 2010	0.16	0.22 B	0.35	(5)	0.28	0.74 AB	1.39	(7)	0.71	0.98 A	1.23	(14)	†
%MeHg	% of THg	2009, 2010	1.26	1.40	1.54	(2)	0.31	0.53	0.94	(7)	0.51	0.69	0.99	(8)	NS
k_{meth}	per day	2010	0.01	0.01	0.01	(2)	0.01	0.01	0.02	(6)	0.00	0.01	0.01	(7)	NS
MPP	pg/g/d dw	2010	0.64	0.79	0.95	(2)	1.42	2.39	3.96	(6)	0.34	1.27	3.68	(7)	NS
K_d[THg]	L/kg	2010	4.47	4.61	4.75	(2)	4.50	4.71	4.93	(6)	4.77	4.88	5.08	(7)	NS
K_d[MeHg]	L/kg	2010	3.26	3.30	3.33	(2)	2.92	3.20	3.37	(6)	3.04	3.24	3.65	(7)	NS
Pore-water mercury parameters															
pw.THg	ng/L	2009, 2010	0.26	0.70 B	1.35	(5)	1.15	1.32 A	8.68	(7)	0.94	1.72 AB	2.30	(13)	NS
pw MeHg	ng/L	2009, 2010	0.06	0.10 B	0.10	(5)	0.19	0.52 A	1.90	(7)	0.07	0.29 AB	0.55	(13)	†
pw%MeHg	% of THg	2009, 2010	10.8	21.1	29.4	(3)	17.7	30.2	38.7	(6)	7.97	24.0	27.3	(9)	NS
Biota total mercury															
Oligochaete	ng/g ww	2009	18.3	19.5 B	21.6	(5)	24.7	32.2 AB	40.6	(8)	27.1	31.3 A	38.7	(11)	†
Crayfish	ng/g ww	2009, 2011	50.0	59.3 B	64.3	(12)	76.5	95.0 A	111	(25)	69.2	74.1 AB	105	(14)	†
White sucker	ng/g ww	2009, 2011	119	132 B	134	(7)	99.2	153 B	211	(7)	182	251 A	343	(9)	†
Smallmouth bass	ng/g ww	2009, 2011	390	418 B	421	(10)	393	528 B	604	(21)	583	629 A	639	(17)	†
Sediment sequential extractions															
F1: water	ng/g dw	2010	0.03	0.03	0.04	(2)	0.02	0.04	0.44	(6)	0.03	0.05	0.06	(7)	NS
	% of THg	2010	0.09	0.10	0.11	(2)	0.01	0.02	0.09	(6)	0.02	0.02	0.03	(7)	NS
F2: 0.1 M acetic acid	ng/g dw	2010	0.02	0.02	0.03	(2)	0.02	0.04	0.05	(6)	0.02	0.02	0.02	(7)	NS
	% of THg	2010	0.07	0.08	0.09	(2)	0.01	0.02	0.03	(6)	0.01	0.01	0.02	(7)	NS
F3: 1.0 M KOH	ng/g dw	2010	23.4	27.3	31.3	(2)	63.5	82.6	106	(6)	55.7	67.7	92.2	(7)	NS
	% of THg	2010	87.2	87.6	88.1	(2)	33.8	47.4	67.7	(6)	41.2	45.0	54.6	(7)	NS

Table 5. Kruskal-Wallis rank sum test results comparing data grouped by sample distance from a former chloralkali site on the Androscoggin River in Berlin, New Hampshire.—Continued

[The nonparametric Kruskal-Wallis rank sum (KWRS) test comparison of medians grouped by distance from a former chloralkali site. The reference reach (AR2) is 16 kilometers (km) upstream from the former chloralkali site; near-stream reaches (AR3–AR6) are 0 to 4 km downstream from the former chloralkali site; far-stream reaches (AR7–AR9) are 8 to 16 km downstream from the former chloralkali site. The first quartile (25th percentile (%)), median (50th %), and third quartile (75th %) are shown, along with results from all mercury metric comparisons. Only significant results for nonmercury metrics are shown. Tukey multiple-comparison test was used to determine rankings on data KWRS indicated as significant. Letters A and B, indicate which medians are different. A medians are statistically different than B medians, and AB medians are not statistically different than A or B. Parameter notation definitions are listed in table 2. dw, dry weight; EPT, Ephemeroptera, Plecoptera, Trichoptera; g/cm³, grams per cubic centimeter; L/kg, liters per kilogram; mg, milligrams; mL/cm³, milliliters per cubic centimeter; μm, micrometers; mv, millivolts; N, (number of observations); ng/g, nanograms per gram; ng/L, nanograms per liter; NS, nonsignificant differences between groupings at a probability level of p less than 0.05; pg/g/d, picograms per gram per day; THg, total mercury; ww, wet weight; <, less than; †, significant differences between groupings at a probability level of p less than 0.05]

Parameter	Units of measurement	Year	Reference stream reach				Near stream reaches				Far stream reaches				KWRS
			25th %	Median	75th %	N	25th %	Median	75th %	N	25th %	Median	75th %	N	
							Sediment sequential extractions—Continued								
F4: 12 M HNO₃	ng/g dw	2010	2.69	2.98	3.26	(2)	48.0	78.1	145	(6)	53.1	66.6	82.5	(7)	NS
	% of THg	2010	9.36	9.83	10.3	(2)	30.3	46.4	61.3	(6)	43.3	50.0	53.7	(7)	NS
F5: aqua regia	ng/g dw	2010	0.62	0.74	0.86	(2)	3.15	3.36	26.6	(6)	3.49	5.02	6.53	(7)	NS
	% of THg	2010	2.29	2.35	2.40	(2)	2.05	2.40	5.13	(6)	2.42	3.33	4.68	(7)	NS
							Sediment nonmercury parameters								
Sediment E_h	mv	2010	86	104 AB	108	(2)	22	85 B	121	(2)	91	136 A	175	(28)	†
Bulk density	g/cm³ ww	2010	1.32	1.37 B	1.46	(8)	1.48	1.55 A	1.69	(8)	1.44	1.54 AB	1.66	(28)	†
% fines	% <63 μm	2010	63	72 A	75	(8)	26	47 B	56	(8)	29	42 B	57	(28)	†
Porosity	mL/cm³ ww	2010	0.64	0.72 A	0.74	(8)	0.52	0.59 B	0.64	(8)	0.53	0.59 B	0.65	(28)	†
pct.DW	% of wet wt	2009, 2010	43	46 B	56	(11)	56	61 A	70	(25)	56	61 A	67	(35)	†
							Sediment toxicity								
H.azteca survival	%	2009, 2010	78	80	80	(5)	77	79	86	(5)	72	80	84	(14)	NS
H.azteca biomass	mg dw	2009, 2010	0.38	0.39	0.40	(5)	0.43	0.43	0.49	(5)	0.33	0.42	0.50	(14)	NS
C.dilutus survival	%	2009, 2010	70	76	83	(5)	66	80	88	(5)	60	73	76	(14)	NS
C.dilutus biomass	mg dw	2009, 2010	0.44	0.50	1.25	(5)	1.25	1.29	1.48	(5)	0.30	0.67	1.19	(14)	NS
							Pore-water toxicity								
C.tentans survival	%	2009, 2010	80	90	100	(5)	48	85	95	(5)	83	90	99	(14)	NS
H.azteca survival	%	2009, 2010	70	80	80	(5)	95	100	100	(5)	90	95	100	(14)	NS
							Invertebrate metrics								
Abundance		2009	288	316	486	(3)	69.5	587	1,510	(3)	322	604	890	(6)	NS
Total taxa		2009	14	14	15	(3)	9.4	11	13	(3)	11	13	13	(6)	NS
EPT taxa		2009	16	16	16	(3)	13	14	15	(3)	13	17	19	(6)	NS

Table 6   49

Table 6. Sequential extraction results for surface sediment, Androscoggin River, Coos County, New Hampshire.

[Surface sediment encompasses 0- to 10-centimeter (cm) interval. See table 3 for details on the specific fraction number (F#) and associated dominant mercury species extracted. THg, total mercury; ng/g, nanograms per gram; --, no data]

F#	THg, in ng/g dry weight			THg, average, in percent
	Replicate 1	Replicate 2	Average	
AR2–4				
F1	0.02	0.07	0.05	0.12
F2	0.03	0.02	0.03	0.07
F3	34.2	36.2	35.2	88.6
F4	3.79	3.29	3.54	8.9
F5	0.96	1	0.98	2.46
Total	39	40.5	39.8	100
AR2–5				
F1	0.02	--	0.02	0.08
F2	0.02	--	0.02	0.09
F3	19.4	--	19.4	86.8
F4	2.41	--	2.41	10.8
F5	0.5	--	0.5	2.24
Total	22.4	--	22.4	100
AR4–1				
F1	0.83	0.96	0.89	0.11
F2	0.03	0.07	0.05	0.01
F3	62.8	57.6	60.2	7.64
F4	338	1,020	680	86.3
F5	37.8	56.4	47.1	5.97
Total	439	1,140	788	100
AR4–2				
F1	0.56	0.59	0.58	0.44
F2	0.02	0.02	0.02	0.02
F3	35.2	47.9	41.6	31.9
F4	78.5	91.4	84.9	65.1
F5	3.66	3.17	3.41	2.62
Total	118	143	130	100
AR5–1				
F1	0.02	--	0.02	0.01
F2	0.03	--	0.03	0.02
F3	111	--	111	71.9
F4	40.2	--	40.2	26.1
F5	3.1	--	3.1	2.01
Total	154	--	154	100
AR5–2				
F1	0.05	--	0.05	0.01
F2	0.1	--	0.1	0.03
F3	131	--	131	39.7
F4	165	--	165	49.9
F5	34.3	--	34.3	10.4
Total	331	--	331	100

Table 6.   Sequential extraction results for surface sediment, Androscoggin River, Coos County, New Hampshire.
—Continued

[Surface sediment encompasses 0- to 10-centimeter (cm) interval. See table 3 for details on the specific fraction number (F#) and associated dominant mercury species extracted. THg, total mercury; ng/g, nanograms per gram; --, no data]

F#	THg, in ng/g dry weight			THg, average, in percent
	Replicate 1	Replicate 2	Average	
AR6–2				
F1	0.03	--	0.03	0.03
F2	0.04	--	0.04	0.05
F3	73.5	--	73.5	77.6
F4	19.1	--	19.1	20.2
F5	2.06	--	2.06	2.18
Total	94.7	--	94.7	100
AR6–3				
F1	0.01	--	0.01	0.01
F2	0.01	--	0.01	0.01
F3	91.8	--	91.8	55.2
F4	71.3	--	71.3	42.8
F5	3.3	--	3.3	1.98
Total	166	--	166	100
AR7–1				
F1	0.07	--	0.07	0.05
F2	0.02	--	0.02	0.01
F3	56.3	--	56.3	38.2
F4	87.2	--	87.2	59.1
F5	3.9	--	3.9	2.65
Total	147	--	147	100
AR7–2				
F1	0.05	--	0.05	0.03
F2	0.02	--	0.02	0.01
F3	114	--	113.5	69.5
F4	43.8	--	43.8	26.8
F5	5.85	--	5.85	3.58
Total	163	--	163	100
AR8–4				
F1	0.02	--	0.02	0.01
F2	0.03	--	0.03	0.02
F3	70.9	--	70.9	50.4
F4	66.6	--	66.6	47.4
F5	3.08	--	3.08	2.19
Total	141	--	141	100
AR8–5				
F1	0.03	--	0.03	0.02
F2	0.02	--	0.02	0.02
F3	55.1	--	55.1	44.1
F4	62.4	--	62.4	50
F5	7.2	--	7.2	5.77
Total	125	--	125	100

Table 6   51

Table 6. Sequential extraction results for surface sediment, Androscoggin River, Coos County, New Hampshire.
—Continued

[Surface sediment encompasses 0- to 10-centimeter (cm) interval. See table 3 for details on the specific fraction number (F#) and associated dominant mercury species extracted. THg, total mercury; ng/g, nanograms per gram; --, no data]

F#	THg, in ng/g dry weight			THg, average, in percent
	Replicate 1	Replicate 2	Average	
AR9–5				
F1	0.01	--	0.01	0.02
F2	0.02	--	0.02	0.05
F3	28.7	--	28.7	58.9
F4	19.2	--	19.2	39.3
F5	0.86	--	0.86	1.77
Total	48.8	--	48.8	100
AR9–6				
F1	0.05	--	0.05	0.03
F2	0.02	--	0.02	0.01
F3	67.7	--	67.7	45
F4	77.8	--	77.8	51.7
F5	5.02	--	5.02	3.33
Total	151	--	151	100
AR9–7				
F1	0.1	--	0.1	0.02
F2	0.02	--	0.02	0
F3	120	--	119.8	24.2
F4	276	--	276	55.8
F5	98.7	--	98.7	20
Total	494	--	494	100

Appendix 1.   Quality Assurance and Control at the U.S. Geological Survey Laboratory in Menlo Park, California

Tables

Appendix 1.   Quality Assurance and Control at the U.S. Geological Survey Laboratory in Menlo Park, California

Quality assurance (QA) and quality control (QC) results for all parameters assayed by the U.S. Geological Survey (USGS) Western Region Research Laboratory in Menlo Park, Calif., are listed below.

Holding Times

All assays were conducted within the prescribed holding times, as established by either the U.S. Environmental Protection Agency (USEPA), the U.S. Geological Survey (USGS), or peer-reviewed studies from the literature (Horvat and others, 1993; Parker and Bloom, 2005; table 1–1). In the case of studies published in the literature, the USGS laboratory takes a conservative prescribed holding time approach by setting sample holding limits lower than the published study results.

Blanks

Method blanks were run to assess contamination introduced in the laboratory. In most cases, values from the method blanks were below our method detection limit (table 1–2), indicating that the methods and equipment used were free of (or did not introduce) contamination. The exceptions were for pore-water dissolved organic carbon (pw.DOC) and chloride (pw.Cl) where small amounts of the analyte were detected.

Laboratory Replicates

Laboratory analytical replicates represent multiple samples taken from the same container of site-specific sediment as a measure of both sample homogeneity and laboratory reproducibility. At least one analytical replicate was analyzed for each sediment and pore-water parameter; the results are listed in table 1–3.

Matrix Spike Samples

Matrix spike percent recoveries were evaluated to determine acceptable accuracy based on method-specific percent recoveries, which are generally set to be 75- to 125-percent recovery for the laboratory's control limit (table 1–4). Typically when spikes are reported below this accepted range, they indicate a low bias, and when reported above this range, they indicate a high bias. However, if the spike concentration was low compared with the sample concentration, a poor recovery is not in itself indicative of a QC problem. Further, not all sediment parameters are amenable to matrix spikes. For example, the addition of mercuric chloride to sediment quickly partitions itself between tin-reducible and nonreducible pools and thus cannot be used as a reliable matrix spike for the reactive divalent mercury $(Hg(II)_R)$ assay. Similarly, there is no commercially available material that can mimic the operationally defined amorphous ferric iron $(Fe(III)_a)$ sediment pool, and thus the $Fe(III)_a$ assay is not subject to a matrix spike assay.

Certified Reference Material

Certified reference material (CRM) is available for only a limited number of the analytes assayed in the study of the Androscoggin River, specifically for sediment total mercury (THg) and methylmercury (MeHg). Like matrix spikes, CRM recoveries were evaluated to determine acceptable accuracy based on method-specific percent recoveries, which are generally set to be 75 to 125 percent for the laboratory's control limit. CRM recovery results for THg and MeHg are listed in table 1–5.

Appendix 2.   Surface-Water, Pore-Water, Sediment, Invertebrate, and Biota Data

Data in the following tables are for whole (unsieved) streambed-sediment, filtered pore-water, and filtered and unfiltered surface-water samples. Pore-water samples were collected directly from the streambed using a push-point sampler and peristaltic pump.

Tables